D1603019

COMBAT SHOOTING
FOR POLICE

A Monograph in

THE POLICE SCIENCE SERIES

Edited by

V. A. Leonard

Professor of Police Administration
Washington State University
Pullman, Washington

COMBAT SHOOTING
FOR POLICE

Second Edition

By

PAUL B. WESTON

Professor of Criminal Justice
California State University
Sacramento, California

CHARLES C THOMAS • PUBLISHER
Springfield • Illinois • U.S.A.

Published and Distributed Throughout the World by

CHARLES C THOMAS ● PUBLISHER

Bannerstone House

301-327 East Lawrence Avenue, Springfield, Illinois, U.S.A.

© *1960 and 1978, by* CHARLES C THOMAS ● PUBLISHER

ISBN 0-398-03747-7

Library of Congress Catalog Card Number: 77-17817

First Edition, First Printing, 1960
First Edition, Second Printing, 1967
First Edition, Third Printing, 1970
First Edition, Fourth Printing, 1972
First Edition, Fifth Printing, 1975
Second Edition, 1978

With THOMAS BOOKS *careful attention is given to all details of
manufacturing and design. It is the Publisher's desire to present books that
are satisfactory as to their physical qualities and artistic possibilities and
appropriate for their particular use.* THOMAS BOOKS *will be true to those
laws of quality that assure a good name and good will.*

Printed in the United States of America
R-2

Library of Congress Cataloging in Publication Data

Weston, Paul B
    Combat shooting for police.

    (Police science series)
    Bibliography: p.
    Includes index.
    1. Pistols. 2. Pistol shooting. 3. Police--Equip-
ment and supplies. I. Title. II. Series.
HV7936.E7W47 1978   683'.43   77-17817
ISBN 0-398-03747-7

PREFACE

THE first edition of *Combat Shooting for Police* was published in 1960. At that time, most of my shooting background was in New York. I shot as a member of the New York National Guard team and also participated in competitive shooting as a member of the New York City Police Department Pistol Team. At one time, my experience was primarily on the target range, but as the officer in charge of the New York City Police Department Firearms Unit I reoriented myself and thousands of fellow New York police to combat shooting, switching from bull's-eye to combat silhouette targets. Since leaving New York City I have been in Florida and California. I have fired on police ranges in both states and have taught basic and advanced gunnery at California State University at Sacramento, California.

The second edition of *Combat Shooting for Police* updates material from the first edition and includes several new chapters on combat automatic pistols, combat tactics, and selecting the combat revolver or automatic pistol. In addition, the how-to of combat shooting in all of the combat-shooting positions has been revised in accordance with new developments and techniques.

I thank the many persons who have helped in the preparation of this book. I trust all of them know I deeply appreciate their assistance.

P.B.W.

CONTENTS

COMBAT SHOOTING
FOR POLICE

Chapter 1

COMBAT EFFECTIVENESS

THE objective of combat shooting is to deliver directed or aimed fire at an armed opponent as rapidly as possible while offering minimum target area for return fire. The interrelationship of these factors is readily discernable. Inaccurate fire is useless; speed is always to be considered when an opponent is slinging lead; and it is stupid not to seek every means to diminish the target at which an armed criminal may shoot.

Any state, municipality, or other agency of government that employs peace officers and arms them with firearms has the responsibility for training such officers in the rudiments of defensive firing, but also in training such officers to immediately recognize situations that warn of potential combat and the circumstances under which an officer is legally entitled to use his weapon in self-defense, or for other justifiable purposes. This is a coresponsibility. The law enforcement agency trains its personnel to recognize potential combat situations before their opponent seizes the initiative; and the individual peace officer improves on his basic marksmanship training, both on and off duty.

Under civil law, it is considered municipal negligence for any agency of government to fail to effectively train police officers in the safe handling and accurate firing of their revolvers *before* they are assigned to duty.[1,2] Under moral law, it is criminal negligence when an officer fails to build upon this basic training and develop an ability to defend himself.

THE CRIMINAL HAS THE INITIAL ADVANTAGE

The criminal's greatest asset is that he can make up his mind to kill without warning or provocation. He is on the other side of the law and is not bound to remain within legal limits of gunfight behavior. As he slides his weapon out of his pocket or waistband, he has made up his mind to kill. In questioning some of these criminals who survived police combat, it is remarkable that most of them admitted this preparation to kill. A few of their remarks were, "I cocked the hammer back slow, under my coat, so he wouldn't hear the click as he came abreast of us in the car." "I held the gun just behind the wallet as I reached out to hand it to him." "I asked Joe to stand sideways so my hand and gun were behind his back as the cop approached us. When he got close, Joe stepped out of the way. . ."

On the other hand, a police officer must wait for some overt act on the part of the criminal. This act, however, does not have to be a weapon displayed in a hostile manner. It is sufficient for a policeman to start into action, to be alerted that gunplay is imminent, when the criminal makes some motion that a reasonable man would interpret as an attempt to apply armed force against the officer or one in his company. This may not be enough to warrant the officer in shooting, but it is certainly enough to warrant drawing a weapon and preparing to use it.

For some reason, many police seem to believe it is "chicken" to draw a gun. The killers of policemen now range from crazy youths to senile, psychotic old men, and I fail to envisage any situation in which a police officer is not justified in drawing his weapon and learning more about the situation under gun muzzle control, as long as he has reasonable grounds to believe his opponent may be armed and intends to use his or her weapon against the officer.

The normal day of a policeman is usually spent in helping others: a long succession of giving information, finding parents of lost children or children for parents, helping at accident scenes, and adjudicating disputes. In comparison to his total hours of duty, a police officer spends very little time making arrests or even coming into contact with criminals.

A police officer does not carry a revolver or pistol for aggression. The handgun would not be selected as a service weapon if the foremost concern of the policeman was battle. A policeman carries a weapon as the safeguard of a person trying his best to carry out his normally peaceful day's work but aware that he or she may have need of this weapon without much advance notice.

Uncertainty is not the best frame of reference from which to resolve an armed conflict in favor of the police officer. There seems to be a strong instinctive block in the thinking of many police officers. They fail to comprehend the suddenness with which a situation can develop. They fail to recognize the inherent advantage of the criminal in his conflict with the police.

A few policemen on traffic duty in remote areas have developed the technique of drawing their revolver and holding it behind their citation clipboard as they approach a suspicious car. If their suspicions are not confirmed, a slight turn of their body aids in concealing the gun as they tuck it back into their holster. Other officers have developed similar techniques. In New York City, an officer on narcotic squad duty had his revolver holstered in an underarm briefcase, with a convenient side opening to permit him to slide his hand onto the grip of the gun. In Miami, an open paper bag served another officer. While in Portland, Oregon, a detective carried a small five-shot gun in a glove which he held "carelessly" in his hand.

All these techniques are in reality devices to combat the mental attitude of the killer-criminal, to give the policeman a more equal chance to combat a man who not only has his mind made up to kill but upon whom the law bestows the right to attempt it before a policeman can legally attempt to stop him by armed force.

Sometimes it is difficult to put a concept into words readily understandable by most individuals. My difficulty in teaching classes of police recruits rested upon the fact that I did not want them shooting a suspect who "reached into his back pocket for a handkerchief," yet I did not want to assist in shaping a mental attitude that would not adjust to a situation in which an opponent must be killed in self defense — or adjust too slowly. My example was a man named Conrad Jensen. A high-ranking police officer of New York's "finest," he was at the same time a member of our pistol team and a Baptist lay evangelist who spent his spare time reloading cartridges and speaking on the Bible and moral regeneration.

Jensen was a fine example of a man who discharged his duties first as a Christian, then as a policeman. He had, however, also trained himself to shoot accurately when shooting was necessary to overcome resistance. Jensen frequently instructed the patrolmen under his command, "The only time to use force is to overcome resistance, but in that case, a policeman has a legitimate right and a duty to use any method to protect himself." I have never found any better words to express this critical point.

DEFENSIVE FIRING

Almost all police combat shooting is pointed toward defensive firing situations. The police officer faced with a tactical situation, requiring him to defend himself is the best judge of which type of fire may save his life. In such situations, a slight error in judgment can have fatal results, and it is up to the officer himself to make what is usually a split-second decision. On the other hand, the police training officer has a responsibility to acquaint officers with all types of combat shooting and to provide the opportunity for practice under good coaches. Where a department is too small to warrant the assignment of an officer to training duty, the responsibility rests with the chief.

Modern combat shooting in a defensive firing situation is usually double-action directed fire from the hip or point-shoulder shooting, in which the gun is brought up to the shoulder level and pointed at the target. Both positions offer rapidity in getting the first shot off, and the double-action type of fire offers a means of "rapping off" the successive shots with some speed as the gun is cocked and fired in one continuous motion of the trigger finger. Both positions waive the use of the sights for rapid recovery from the recoil and the discharge of another shot with as little time loss as possible.

From the two basic positions, the shooter may find that dropping to a kneeling position offers a lesser target to his opponent and that it is possible to utilize the free hand to support the gun arm for greater accuracy and speedy recovery from the effect of recoil.

If time permits, the officer confronted by an armed opponent can drop into a deeper kneeling position or go into a sitting or prone position. All offer lesser target areas and greater stability in descending order — as the shooter gets closer to the ground.

It is generally true that greater accuracy is secured as the fire is slowed down and more time is taken to fire each shot, but in defensive firing situations, the officer whose life is at stake must weigh the problem of accuracy versus speed.

Possibly the greatest enemy of successful defensive shooting is the empty gun. As a shooter and policeman of over twenty years experience, I know of no situation which gives me greater concern than the modern tendency to teach a policeman to empty his gun. Double-action shooting can empty a gun with great speed. If it is done without the accuracy necessary to cope with the situation, then the police officer is in trouble. I do not care how fast officers can be taught to reload a weapon; if an opponent still has cartridges to shoot and the policeman must reload, the situation cannot be worsened. For the policeman to live, the gunman's weapon has to misfire or his bullets miss their target.

I once listened to a firearms training officer of a large Eastern city deliver a lecture on shooting. He spoke glibly of the Practical Police Course, of tactical situations requiring defensive firing, of night firing, and other aspects of firearms training. Not once did he mention the great need for accuracy of fire, although he did deplore the need of training men in slow firing shooting.

A great truth in pistol shooting, regardless of whether the fire is directed at a target or an armed criminal, is that only the hits count. If the situation demanded it I would "sweep off" two or three fast shots from the hip, then "point-directional" one or two more, and if these shots did not silence my opponent, I would aim and fire. I think my mind would be working on a single thought: "Make them count; an empty gun is useless."

BULL'S-EYE TARGET TRAINING

It is difficult to conceive of a method of teaching combat shooting without some basic training on the bull's-eye target. The accuracy of fire that may some day be the difference between life and death should be a basic requirement before any speed of fire is attempted. It is ridiculous to move into any type of combat shooting until the shooter has learned the fundamentals of pistol shooting, and unless these fundamentals are learned in the first instance, they may never be acquired.

The fundamentals of gripping, sighting, and aiming and trigger squeeze can be taught on any target, from blank white paper squares to blackened silhouettes. The bull's-eye target, however, offers an opportunity to evaluate a shooter's ability more readily than these other targets.

Another advantage to bull's-eye targets is the fact that they tend to bring out a latent tendency to shoot poorly. Concentration on hitting the center leads to poor sight alignment and incorrect aiming, and the same attempt to be too precise results in attempts to make the gun go off with a sudden pressure of the trigger, and this "jerk" moves the gun away from the target center. Once out in the open, any fault can be corrected, and it is more desirable to have these faults develop during the initial training stage, when correction is not too difficult, than to have them crop up after lengthy periods of indoctrination in faulty habits. These faults can be diagnosed by "reading" the target. Hits tend to groupings characteristic of the fault.

The scores ascertained from bull's-eye targets lend themselves to ready classification of shooters, based on their ability to group their hits. An individual shooter (or a police unit) can arbitrarily establish any limit as a threshold to combat training, but this minimum score should be sufficiently high to insure that the shooter has learned the fundamentals. This is usually around 70 percent average in slow fire on targets with a standard "time and rapid fire" bull's-eye of about 3 inches in diameter and fired at the standard distance of 25 yards.

A good minimal distance for bull's-eye training is 25 yards. Fifteen yards is acceptable for the initial ten rounds of indoctrination firing but is too short for aimed fire to be meaningful in evaluating performance with a handgun.

SAFETY

The modern revolver or automatic pistol is more powerful, more accurate, and more easily handled than ever before. It is a weapon designed to kill. It must be handled in such a manner that its lethal power is never used accidentally. It is designed primarily to kill in defense of life or property, and it can, of course, be used for any intentional killing, but it is a tragedy when a revolver kills or injures a person as a result of an accident.

I have investigated many accidents with firearms. All of them could have been prevented. It is far better never to own a gun than to be the cause of someone's death by careless handling of one.

The following ten rules for safety are the general rules a shooter must know and must practice until they become fixed habits:

1. Always unload your gun if it is to be left where someone else may handle it.
2. Actually go through the motions of unloading your gun every time you pick it up. Look at the cylinder of a revolver and look into the chamber of an automatic pistol to make certain it is empty. Check the magazines of automatic pistols to make certain they are taken out of the gun or that they are empty or both.
3. Develop safe habits whenever the gun is removed from the holster or the gun and holster placed in a desk or locker.
4. Extend the trigger finger outside of the trigger guard* until ready to fire.
5. Never point a gun at anyone you do not intend to shoot, and keep the muzzle pointed in a "safe" direction.
6. Always keep the cylinder swung out or the slide open when the gun is out of the holster but not in actual use.

---

*See Appendices A and B for the names and locations of the major parts of revolvers and pistols.

7. Know your gun, ammunition, and holster.
8. Keep your fingers away from the muzzle (watch this on the 2-inch barrel guns).
9. Quick-draw practice is hazardous — safety first.
10. Be certain wax bullets are not ball ammunition.

REFERENCES

1. Rummel, B.: Police firearms training: An inquiry into the governmental duty to provide adequate training. *The American Rifleman, III (8):*17, August, 1963.
2. Peer v. City of Newark, 71 NJ Super 12, 176 A.2d 249, (Nov., 1961).

Chapter 2

DEFENSIVE DIRECTED FIRE

DIRECTED fire is that fire in which the officer does not have time to use the sights of a weapon to aim as he fires. It is utilized when an armed opponent is firing at the officer at close range. It presupposes a shortage of time, and it is the answer to a police officer's problems when the chips are down and life can be forfeit.

Directed fire may be delivered from either the hip or the shoulder level. Hip shooting gives great rapidity in getting off the first shot, while point shooting from the shoulder usually means greater accuracy. The officer concerned is the only one to evaluate the situation and determine whether he or she can afford the luxury of moving into a point-shoulder position. Life is at stake and only the threatened officer can make this decision.

ROOM-SIZED SHOOTING

As the distance to the target is increased, it is only natural that the accuracy of directed fire from the hip diminishes. Hip shooting is meant for what might be termed room-sized situations. It is effective within the confines of a small store, a narrow hallway, any room, or when what appeared to be a harmless traffic violator piles out of his car and starts a gun moving in the direction of the approaching police officers.

In determining the distance at which directed fire from the hip should be practiced, the Federal Bureau of Investigation settled upon 7 yards or 21 feet for this phase of their fine Practical Pistol Course (PPC). Pace off any room, store, or hallway, and see just how far — rather how close — 7 yards seems to be.

The apparent closeness of this range is deceptive, in that it appears impossible to miss an opponent. However, any individual who has gone through the 7-yard hip shooting stage of

11

the PPC without any previous coaching can usually testify to the fact that the target can be missed — and more than once.

I once had to testify for the city of New York in a Supreme Court case involving police firearms training and room-sized shooting. The police officer had been sent by a police radio alarm to a small store on a "Signal 30" — felony in progress — and had his service revolver in his hand as he entered the store. It was an almost empty room; at the far end, facing each other across a table, stood two men. The one on the officer's right had a gun in his hand and the man opposite him had both arms raised in the air in the universal gesture of surrender. The officer opened fire on the criminal, and shot and killed the victim!

In another case, three officers fired eighteen bullets — all of them unloaded their guns — at a parolee fleeing in a stolen car, but unfortunate enough to be stalled in a tie-up of New York's traffic in front of the Criminal Courts building. One officer was no farther away than the right front fender of the stolen vehicle, but the parolee was not touched by any of the fire, although all eighteen bullets did hit the car.

These stories are unbelievable, but all are true. Possibly, it is true stories such as these, predating my entrance into police work in 1936, that caused oldtimers in the police firearms field to insist that every shot be an aimed shot. However, we now know hip shooting can be directed with great accuracy and considered a necessary phase of police training in combat shooting — perhaps the most important phase of the entire shooting program.

THE HIP SHOOTING POSITION

The eyes, the elbow, and the wrist are the keys to good direction of fire from the hip position. The gun must become an extension of the wrist; the elbow must act to join the gun and wrist to the body so that the shooter's muscles respond to visual cues.

The first step in successful hip shooting is to look intently at the area on an opponent or a silhouette target representing an opponent, into which it is desired to place bullets. Look, and the movements of the body can be coordinated to shoot a weapon where you are looking. However, the necessary coordination requires intelligent practice.

The first step is to attempt some kind of coordination practice without the gun. Temporarily, during the training stage, forget about drawing the gun from a holster. The starting position in this initial coordination practice is with the muzzle of the revolver down and pointed just beyond the toes of the shooter, and the practice is concerned with bringing the gun upward and forward into position for an effective first shot.

Try it in front of a mirror with an empty gun. Bring the gun up a few times in what seems to be the normal movement. Now put it down and look at Figure 1. Study the Figure 1 legend and notice how the grip must be tight, with the thumb locked in a downward position; how the wrist must be locked, with the barrel and the forearm horizontal with the ground as the gun moves into firing position, so that it serves as a firm link between the hand grasping the gun and the forearm of the shooter; and how the elbow must be carried well into the body to better serve as a hinge joining the forearm and gun to the body, a hinge which not only must absorb recoil without loss of time in recovery of position, but which must also serve as the mount for the gun.

Study Figure 1 so that an understanding may be possible as to how the tenseness of the grip, the locked wrist, and the elbow behind the gun all contribute to the firmness of the upper arm and shoulder, which in turn makes it possible for the shooter to respond to visual cues with the movements of his entire body. Note the position of each shoulder socket and joint. The right shoulder (of a right-handed person) drops slightly in order to permit him to move his elbow in toward the center of his body. Note the position of the elbow in relation to the hip sockets (Fig. 1).

Notice how the crouch position brings all these critical areas into a better position. Originally, the crouch position was considered the most desirable because it reduced the target area into which the criminal could place hits, but a better understanding

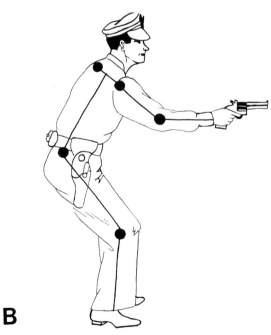

Figure 1A and 1B.

Figure 1A and 1B. The Hip-level Crouch Position. (A) Right elbow is well into the body and behind the gun, and the right shoulder is dropped slightly. (B) Position of major bone joints in the hip-level crouch position. A firm grip, level forearm, and the position of the elbow behind the gun are fundamentals of this position.

Figure 1C. Two-hand Crouch Position. Two-hand shooting steadies the weapon. Nonshooting hand supports the shooting hand when the shooting hand has punched forward into the directed-fire position. Note erect back and line of sight toward target.

of this position has lead to the conclusion that the crouch position tends to more effective control of body movements in response to visual cues.

Standing in front of a mirror, practice going into a fairly deep crouch position as you move your gun up to hip shooting level. Regardless of where you may be looking on the mirror "opponent," normally the resultant point of aim — direction — is fairly low. Remember, the barrel and forearm must be level with the floor. Turn sideways, level the barrel and forearm in the full standing position, and go into a deep crouch. Note how the gun is pointing low again. Now come up about halfway out of the deep crouch and watch how the muzzle comes up within the aiming area. This is the method of controlling vertical changes in directing fire.

The gun, the locked arm, and the entire body are moved upward by flexing the knees to raise the level of fire. In reverse, the same is true when it is necessary to lower the point of impact. Experiment with this a few minutes, learn it, and adjust your visual point of aim to fit the depth of your crouch. This is the key to directing fire at the hip level.

Now, find a friend who will stand to one side as you face the mirror and tell you whether or not your gun barrel and forearm are level with the floor. Drop into position a few times, listen to corrections from your friend, and adjust your forearm and wrist before locking them into position with a tight grip. Flex the knees and move the locked arm and body up and down a few times. Listen to your "coach," and get the feel of a level forearm and gun barrel.

Horizontal alignment can be checked visually, it is merely a case of glancing down and then up to the target rapidly, following the direction in which the barrel is pointed, to see if the weapon is pointed too far to the left or right.

If a tendency to point the gun to the left or right with some consistency becomes evident, check the position of the elbow. An elbow pushed too far into the body — possibly with the shoulder dropped too low — results in the muzzle coming up into position to the right of the target area. On the other hand, when the muzzle seems to come into position to the left of the area at which the shooter is looking, it is likely that the elbow is too far away from the body — too near the right hip socket for a right-handed shooter. If the elbow appears to be in the correct position, it may be necessary to move the feet to correct this condition.

Basically, the shooter should face his target squarely, with his weight slightly toward the balls of his feet but with both heels solidly on the ground. (Then if he or she is hit, he will fall forward into position where he may be able to get in another shot.) Some men find the crouch position slightly more comfortable when they advance the left foot slightly and assume the position of a professional boxer as he spars with an opponent. Whatever the position may be, if the elbow is in a good position, do not move it to secure horizontal correction. It is much more desirable to adjust the feet and learn the position necessary to come up squarely in the center of the target area, where the vision is concentrated.

Care should be exercised that the body is not bent forward solely at the waist in assuming the crouch position (*see* Fig. 1C). There is only a slight leaning forward as the buttocks are dropped down when a shooter's knees are bent, but this position of the upper body remains the same, regardless of the depth of the crouch. Actually, the legs are the major factor in this position from which fire from the hip can be directed with such great accuracy; they form two supports for the position. It is similar to a bipod mount for a machine gun.

Punching the gun hand at the target is helpful at this point. Step away from the mirror, and punch forward with the gun as the crouch position is assumed. If an opponent were close, the gun muzzle would be punched forward to hit him in the center of his body.

This punching technique is quite natural, and its success is based on the natural punching capabilities characteristic of any normal American male. From childhood the boys of this country learn to direct punches, and as they grow up, this ability is cultivated. It is also a major phase of the physical training of police officers. As a result, it is more effective than the "pointing" technique of directing fire, as most people never needed to point with any great degree of accuracy.

The gun is punched up into the field of secondary vision as the shooter looks intently at his target. In cases such as this, the shooter does not actually see it, but he is aware that it is there. If the gun did not point at the target, the shooter would become aware of this fact. It is a visual cue to correct punching techniques. If the shooter consciously looks down at the gun, then his eye control over muscular coordination is ruined.

However, when practice at this position is first attempted, it is a good practice to look down and check the position of the muzzle to see if it is pointed at the target, but then you must return your primary vision to the target. At this same stage of combat shooting, it is also desirable to have a friend check your forearm and barrel to make certain they are level as you move into range practice with live ammunition.

Once the punching or swinging motion is grooved, you may move to the outdoor range. Use the bank of the backstop itself for this initial practice. Place a cartridge box in the sand or earth of the bank at about waist level. In this fashion, you can readily observe the effect of your fire.

This observation of fire is of top importance all the way through hip shooting practice until some real proficiency is attained — some weeks later and only after consistent practice.

The weapon is loaded with one cartridge — one round. The cylinder is closed so that the weapon discharges when the trigger is pulled for the first time, and the muzzle is pointed at the ground in front of the shooter in a "ready" position. This is close to the "in-holster" position, without actually placing the gun in a holster.

At a signal, or your own cue, go into the crouch position and punch the gun up and forward, firing the first shot as the gun levels into position — being careful that the trigger pressure does not disturb the pointing of the weapon. Observe the effect of the fire and determine if the gun had swung up too high or low or too far to either side.

Unload and, if necessary, practice a few swings into position with the empty gun until fairly certain that the swing is grooved. Fire a few more single rounds, interspersing the fire with practice with the empty gun. Now load the six chambers of the revolver, and fire one shot at a time at this latest stage of practice. However, come back to the "in-holster" position between shots, so that each shot is a true "first shot," but fire with sufficient rapidity to get the feel of corrections from shot to shot. Your eye is the key at this stage. Look at the cartridge box, shoot, and observe the place of impact and then adjust to correct as you move into position for the next shot. After a short time, what can only be described as a "feel" develops for this position. It is the pairing of visual cues with muscle impulses, and it comes to most individuals after some practice.

GETTING INTO ACTION

After mastering hip shooting, buckle on a holster and try drawing the empty revolver from the holster. You should move slowly at first, then slightly more rapidly, but never with any sense of hurry. The police officer must get the gun out of the holster but must first get a correct grip on the gun before drawing it. "Slapping leather" is for cowboys or Western gun fighters. Take it slow and easy.

The first objective is to get the correct grip on the gun while it is in the holster. Grip the weapon, draw it out, examine the grip, make minor adjustments, then holster the weapon and repeat the process until the gun can be drawn with the correct grip. This is important (Fig. 2).

Next, coordinate the drawing motion with the punching or swinging motion utilized to get the weapon into position at hip level. This should be one continuous motion, and it has to be performed very slowly at first in order to combine the two motions before any attempt at speed is made.

Speed is not essential in drawing the gun. Ability to secure the correct shooting grip while the gun is in the holster and to come up smoothly to correct shooting position are greater assets than mere speed. In fact, quick or fast draws are overrated in the police business. In most cases, an alert cop either has the gun in his or her hand or half out of the holster.

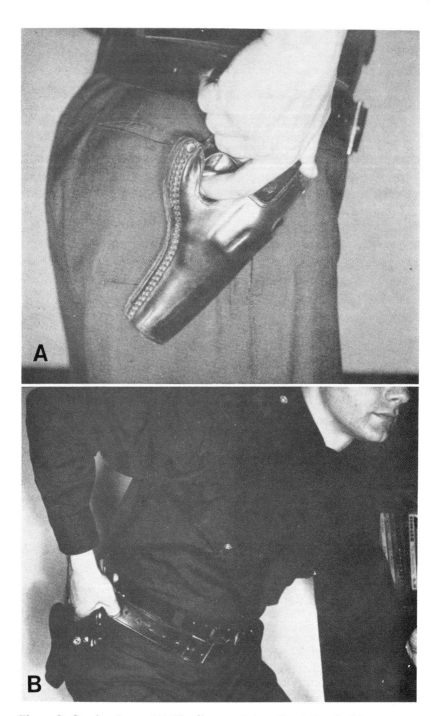

Figure 2. Combat Draw. (A) The fingers of the officer's hand slide under the butt in their normal shooting position and start the gun moving up and forward. As the gun moves, the index finger starts into the trigger guard, and the thumb angles toward its position on the side of the gun. (B) Note that the officer moves into the crouch position as the gun starts to clear the holster.

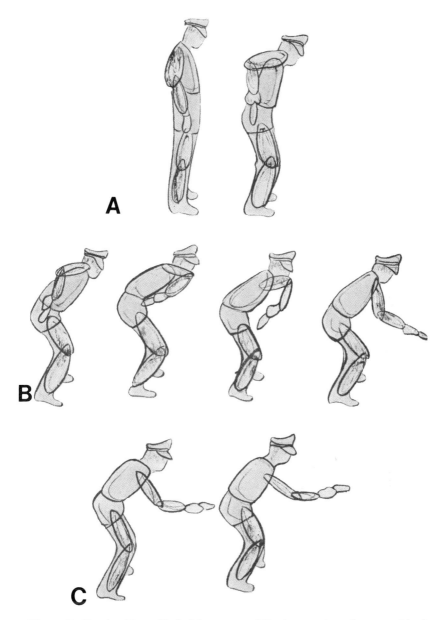

Figure 3. Combat Draw Body Movements. The integration of arm and body movements during a combat quick draw is well illustrated in this sequence of mass-and-motion studies. (A) The officer secures the correct shooting grip, moves his elbow into a high position, flexes his knees, and begins his sidestep. (B) The officer's high elbow acts as a swivel joint to move the gun in a swaybacked arc toward the target. As the gun is moved up and forward, the officer's elbow is dropped down toward a position in front of his right hip. (C) The officer's elbow drops into a position well forward of his hip and directly behind the revolver.

POINT-SHOULDER SHOOTING

In the point-shoulder position, the weapon is not stopped at hip level upon drawing from the holster, but the punching or throwing motion is continued for the full natural extension of the arm. At arm's length, "pointing" is on a par with "punching."

At arm's length, most individuals can shoot more accurately and almost as rapidly as from the hip — as long as they do not look at the sights of the gun.

The primary vision must be concentrated on the target in this position to such an extent that it may be termed *tunnel vision* within its narrowest definition. The gun is well into the field of secondary vision, but the shooter must *look over or around* the weapon if he is to use this position for directed fire similar to shooting from hip level. Once the primary vision is drawn from the target to the sights, then it is aimed fire — and the rate of fire slows down considerably.

It is, of course, not good technical competence to ignore the gun entirely, the shooter should accept visual cues that indicate the gun is pointed to the right or left or the muzzle is far too low or too high. However, these visual cues should be consciously accepted during the initial practice sessions only. I believe that noticing the need for minor corrections leads to looking for them, and the eyes have a more important job in directing fire: to *coordinate the muscular structure of the body in pointing the weapon forward toward the target so that the line of fire will coincide with the line of sight.*

Practice the point-shoulder position in the same manner as the hip shooting position was practiced, but in point-shoulder shooting the services of a friend are no longer needed as the shooter can glance at his gun in order to ascertain where it is pointing.

The welding of the muscular structure of the body into a unit coordinated by vision and a "feel" developed through practicing the point-shoulder shooting position starts with a firm grip and ends with a locked wrist, elbow, and shoulder. The firm grip is the key to a locked wrist, and both of them aid in keeping the elbow and shoulder relatively immobile. In this position, it is much less difficult to keep the elbow and shoulder locked into position than it is in hip shooting, as the arm is fully extended (Fig. 4).

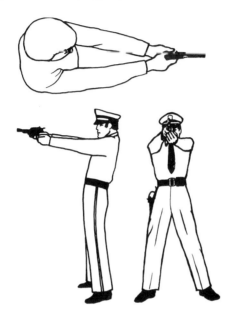

Figure 4. Point-Shoulder Position. Weapon is brought up to just below the line of sight to the target. Both hands grasp the weapon; the free hand joins the shooting hand as the gun is pointed at the target. The gun is centered in front of the body at shoulder level.

TRAVERSE TARGETS

Whenever an officer is confronted with more than one criminal in armed combat he or she will find it necessary to swing from one target to another. Usually, there is little need for vertical correction, as long as the officer is seeking to hit the center of the mass of an opponent's body. In range practice, targets are placed at varying distances apart in order to secure practice at this necessary phase of police combat shooting.

A mirror and a friend who may assist in coaching are both

necessary for initial practice at traversing from one target to another. Stand in front of a mirror, to one side, and ask your friend to stand beside you so that he can also be seen in the mirror. Now drop into the positions described in this chapter, with the initial direction of fire being directed at your own image in the mirror. Now, and very slowly, *swing your entire body* around until the muzzle of your revolver is pointing at the image of your friend in the mirror. Be certain that your wrist is not bent, forearm turned from the elbow, or arm moved at the shoulder.

Try very short traverses at first to get into the swing. Learn the movement, then increase the distance between yourself and your friend as far as mirror and room permit.

NIGHT SHOOTING FROM D.D.F. POSITIONS

Directed Defensive Firing (D.D.F.) positions are ideally suited to night firing. Combat situations in which there is sufficient light (and time) to pick up the sights and go into aimed fire or in which the use of a flashlight would not be suicidal, are discussed in Chapter 5. Directed fire is ideal for situations in which time is of the essence and visibility is limited.

In directed fire, the officer punches or points his or her gun, and once this technique is learned — and the officer has sufficient practice to retain his learning — then the fire can be delivered as accurately in very poor light as it can be delivered in bright sunlight.

Lighting is a factor concerned with defensive directed firing positions that has been sadly neglected, and it is a vital one. The use of a flashlight in a dark cellar while searching for an armed opponent might well be a death warrant.

A policeman in New York City went into a cellar in New York's Negro ghetto, Harlem, and stopped a few feet inside the door — he could not see. He moved aside away from the slight light coming through the door and debated turning on his flashlight, but some instinctive impulse kept him from moving his finger on the flashlight button. Just then, he heard a voice from the other side of the cellar, "Come and get it, you m ____ f ———— cop."

His report of the incident concluded, ". . . and I fired at the noise and moved along the wall. My fire was returned and I emptied my gun at the flashes. John C ———— , black male, thirty-five years of age, dead on arrival of assisting officers."

Another night firing technique that may some day save an officer's life was told to me quite casually. I had the Detective's Training School in New York's Police Academy for a short time, and our last session was shooting at targets in a darkened room. The lights were on when the detective entered the range area, and he could see his opponent (a silhouette target) at the far end of the range, but he could not draw his gun or stop walking until the lights went out. This simulated a situation in which an armed adversary or an accomplice put the lights out as the detective moved into the room to make an arrest.

In one of the classes, we had an amazing score and an amazing shot group. The first shot had been low, but all the shots were well into the mass of the target and all grouped closely together. Later, out of curiousity, I called this individual's command and spoke to him on the phone. I told him what was on my mind and he laughed. "That's an old cop's trick," he told me. "The man that broke me in years ago told me about it. You shoot fast and use the light from the flashes. Maybe I don't see the sights, but I could see the gun and I could see the target."

Since night shooting is required in a very high percentage of combat situations, it is well worth the time spent on practice. I advise using lights to get things set up — and to provide the necessary margin of safety — before going into this type of practice, but then try out directed fire at targets which you cannot see except by a very poor light or the flash of your gun. Later, arrange some kind of audio signal to denote the target and learn to direct fire at a sound.

A length of wire can be hooked up with an old cigarette lighter and a buzzer and an automobile used to actuate this mechanism on an outdoor range. A friend can plug it into the lighter socket on the dashboard of the car for an instant to give you the sound. Another device is very simple, a screw eye in the back of the target, a string, and a weight. Tie the weight (a rock will do) to the string, thread it through the screw eye, and run it back to the firing line. When ready to fire, pull the string far enough back to raise the weight, then drop it, and fire at the noise.

Conclusion

It takes practice to learn directed defensive fire because the key to accuracy is position. The eyes and the body must coordinate, and to "groove" this coordination, the shooter must get the "feel" of the position. There is no other way to describe it; there is no other way to learn it.

If an officer had to select only one type of fire at which to become proficient, I would seriously advise defensive directed fire as his selection. It is the type of fire you must use when an armed opponent is shooting at you.

Remember, in combat situations, an opponent is afraid of the armed police officer and is really slinging lead. The police officer has to shoot equally fast and more accurately to survive. Accuracy without speed may mean a DOA police officer and a spouse living on a pension.

A fact which should not be overlooked in evaluating rapid and directed fire is that it may be the answer to the problem of, "Gimme your gun, Copper." A good defensive firing man can reply, ". . . and here it comes — in six, easy installments."

Chapter 3

"GIMME YOUR GUN, COPPER"

THE scene was a liquor store; the policeman in uniform. He had walked in to query the proprietor as to how late he was going to remain open. A few steps inside the door and he knew something was wrong: The owner failed to sound off in his customary noisy greeting; the "customer" looked strange and tense; and now the customer's, "Gimme your gun, copper." Simultaneously, the policeman realized that the customer had a gun in his hand and it was pointed at him. . . .

Most policemen will not give up their sidearms too easily. It is a tradition of many years to regard such officers with contempt. It is probably very unfair; many officers encounter situations in which their life no doubt would be forfeit if they refused to surrender their weapon. However, police history is replete with incidents of policemen who refused to surrender their revolver and apprehended or killed the criminal who had the drop on them.

A lecture to police officers concerned with surrendering side arms to criminals seems to effect an almost chemical change in the air of the class room. There's fright and fear in the air; and there is a little resentment. The fear seems to foster hostility, and that is directed at the lecturer. Up to this point, most police recruits have looked upon their new profession as a job and resent talk about war. What war? The war between the underworld and the community. Battles are fought every day, the police are the foot soldiers of the community, but unless the officer shoots and kills a criminal, or a criminal shoots a policeman — or disarms him — there is no official communique and little public notice. The battles are still being fought.

The police officer should never forget the fact that the community arms police to defend against the people of the underworld. The police officer is an armed sentry on duty. The

officer must remember that most of the community are unarmed and are easy prey to armed criminals, and the officer
owes a moral duty to the public to not only disarm the criminal
but also to use every means at his disposal to avoid arming him
with another gun.

The crux of talking a criminal out of his gun rests upon
playing on basic fears. Every crook, thug, and hoodlum in the
underworld knows what happens to cop killers. "Bum"
Rogers, a well-known New York hoodlum of the early 1920s,
summed up a misspent life when he told the witnesses as-
sembled for his execution in the death chamber at Sing Sing, "I
never should have killed that cop; that's where all my trouble
started."

One of the facets contributing to the rise of the Mafia in the
American underworld has been their reluctance to kill a police
officer. Armed killers have surrendered to police within moments after a killing, because their "contract" did not include
killing a policeman. "Murder, Inc.," New York's contribution
to the hierarchy of homicide, never ran afoul of a police officer
in over fifty-six killings.

Most of the professionals in the underworld, fences, and
those who shelter criminals for a fee, agree on this point: "Cop
killers are poison."

Policeman A walked into a supermarket "stick-up" early one
morning. Two thugs had captured the manager of the store as
he left his car. The thugs were walking him across the parking
lot to open the store and force him to open the safe, when the
policeman drove up.

"Out of the car," was the first command to the surprised
policeman. "Reach," was the second order. But that is as far as
the cop went. He kept walking toward the group and talking
about what happens to "cop killers"; that juries convict, and
judges say the electric chair is too good for them. Sounds too
simple, too pat, but it has worked in the past, and it functioned
very well in this case. Remember, the criminal is a bit disorgan-
ized at the sudden appearance of the policeman, and while his
first impulse is defensive, any words of the policeman that may
contribute to his disorganization may lead to panic and sur-

render.

As a policeman, you are a member of a club that knows no boundaries anywhere in the world. The police of Georgia seek out a cop killer just as earnestly as the police of foreign countries. "Wanted for killing a police officer" on an FBI wanted bulletin appears to raise hackles on the back of any police officer. Possibly, it is the interrelationship of individuals working in the same vocation that accounts for this attitude, but it may also be the fact that these same wanted notices usually carry the superfluous caution, ". . . armed and dangerous."

The criminal knows that once he kills a policeman that other officers may have a slight tendency to shoot first and ask questions after a short interval. Proof of this fact comes from a man who had just killed a police lieutenant in Bal Harbour, Florida. George Lewis, a policeman in Hollywood, Florida, had been alerted by his dispatcher and stopped the criminal's car in its flight north along U. S. 1A. He approached the car with caution, disarmed the criminal of a gun which was still in place under his left thigh, and held him at gunpoint until the city's "backup" car arrived. George reports that he heard nothing during these few minutes but pleas, "Don't shoot me. I never meant to kill him. Don't shoot me. I never meant to kill him." It was a refrain, repeated over and over.

George still talks about it. He was scared as he pulled the car over: A top pistol shot, but after all, the man he was stopping had just a few minutes earlier fired a fatal bullet into another policeman. I would be scared, too. If Lewis had not been alert enough to cover his man from the first moment of the approach, he might now be dead, but once his opponent capitulated, even George was surprised at the man's panic.

SHOOTING IT OUT

The readiness to shoot it out is a fine thing, but the cop-killer theme can be enlarged upon by the apparent readiness of the policeman to shoot. There may be no need to rush things; possibly, a word to the effect that the criminal should drop his gun and surrender because the cop will get him before he dies may be worth the effort.

Two highly intelligent Sacramento, California, police officers are alive, and with a good "collar" on their record, because they did not rush into a gun battle. A man had robbed a small store and fled up an alley. At the same time, the victim fled out the front door, hollering, "police." Two motorcycle officers were passing at the moment, took it all in, slewed around the corner, and met face-to-face with the robber as he exited from the alley. The robber had a loaded revolver in his hand, but the police approached him from slightly different directions and "talked" him into surrendering, on the theme that "one of us will get you."

A police officer must realize that the criminal may give up but that there are instances in which full panic takes control and he starts blazing away at the officer. The exact circumstance of the moment, the premises concerned, the type of criminal, and his apparent armament are all essential elements in serving to shape the officer's evaluation of the situation.

A cop named Williams, in New York's 20th Precinct, walked into an assault and robbery in a small delicatessen on a Sunday evening and threw himself down behind a counter at the command to halt and give up his gun. He had no time for talking. Williams and his partner faced not one, but three armed men, and when the dust settled, two of the thugs were dead and the other wounded.

Williams and his partner — who rushed in to back him up when he heard the shots rap out — fired twenty-four bullets, both reloading as they scurried around among the salami behind the counter of the delicatessen, and one of the hold-up men also reloaded and fired another clip.

It was a classic tale of New York's West Side but later served me in good stead as I talked to classes of police recruits. The score of this encounter was a good one to count; the police team's only injury was some plaster dust in William's eye — driven in by the impact of a bullet in the plaster wall close to his head.

The premises may offer ideal concealment opportunities for

an officer in the vital moments it takes to draw the revolver and get into action. These facts must be sensed; there is no time to look around and take an appraisal. I queried Patrolman Williams on this point, and he told me, "Chief, I didn't think. I just dove, then I rolled over and got my gun out. I guess the opening was there and I just sensed it, but it was pure reflex action, no conscious thinking, not me."

Something about the criminal may be the deciding factor as to what action is most advantageous for the policeman. The criminal may be very young or very old. He may be indecisive in his actions. My own worst experience in this field concerned a thirteen-year-old boy who held a cocked .22 caliber rifle on my navel as I walked up to him. It was a senseless, stupid act for the boy (he was only guilty of shooting robins in a park), but he became a victim of panic and told me, "Stop, don't move a foot." It's hard to remember exactly what I said, but it was something to the effect of not pointing a gun at anyone and to point it at the ground and open the bolt. His only resistance was to tell me, "It's cocked!" I told him, "That's what worries me; open the bolt." That was it. He opened the bolt and meekly turned over the gun.

Sometimes an officer is threatened by a gun he knows is deadly: his own or his partner's revolver or pistol. In one or two of these instances, the gun threat has been a .357 Magnum, taken away from an officer while struggling with a suspect. In one case, an officer who refused to surrender was shot by his partner's .357 Magnum.

One of the manufacturers of soft body armor suggests to police officers who carry .357 revolvers that they position medium-power rather than Magnum loads in the first two chambers of the revolver's cylinder. In this way, an officer threatened with his own gun — and wearing a bullet-resistant vest — would know that the vest would protect against wounding by the medium-power (.38 Special, for instance) cartridges if their assailant did shoot and aimed for the body rather than the head of the officer.

Joseph Wambaugh's *The Onion Field*[1] is based on a real-life event in Los Angeles in which two armed robbers on parole disarmed one policeman and held him at gunpoint under threat until his partner surrendered. Later, in an onion field in the nearby mountains, one policeman was fatally shot, and the other escaped. The two robbers spent several hours hunting for the escaped officer before fleeing with the revolvers of both officers. Wambaugh's novel not only details this event but also deals with the tragic aftermath: the wreck of the escaped officer's life.

Police management can strongly suggest that officers should not surrender, as surrender is no guarantee of an officer's safety or the safety of a police partner. However, when I looked at the dead men in the Williams delicatessen robbery case, I know I would not have tried to talk them out of anything. They were naturally cold-looking at the moment, as rigor mortis had set in, but in life they had been hard-looking people. Williams must have sensed this, even though he cannot now recall it, just before he hit the deck. This is an evaluation that only the officer at the scene, at the moment of surprise, can make — and it has to be an excellent appraisal.

Conclusion

The officer's critical evaluation of a surrender situation, based on a knowledge of his or her capabilities at defensive shooting and the overall situation, may mean the difference between life or death. Surrender may mean death; refusal to surrender may also mean death.

The confidence that exists when an officer knows he or she can handle a weapon effectively assists that person when decision making must occur rapidly and at a high level of performance for survival.

REFERENCE

1. Wambaugh, J.: *The Onion Field.* New York, Dell, 1974.

Chapter 4

GRIP ... SIGHTS ... AIM ... SQUEEZE

IT is necessary to compartmentalize learning
to shoot. A good coach never throws a great deal of instruc-
tional material at a shooter, because a great majority of people
can only absorb a few things at a time. The basic principles of
shooting a handgun are concerned with how to grip the gun to
the best advantage, the correct manner of aligning the sights,
how to aim, and the mechanics of the critical stage of pistol
and revolver shooting — the trigger-pressure period. These
techniques might also be described as necessary elements with a
high degree of interrelationship. If the shooter's performance of
any of these elements falls below par, then the entire performance of the shooter will be below par.

This is so important to successful shooting that it is vital for
a new shooter to make his own analysis. Why is a good grip
necessary? Why must the sights be aligned correctly? How vital
is the aiming procedure? Can improper methods of pulling the
trigger ruin accuracy of fire? These are questions that a shooter
must answer in his or her own mind in order to fully realize the
importance of each stage in the basic mechanics of shooting
and to recognize the relationship of each element to the whole.
This is almost self-analysis.

The shooter can examine a gun, take a grip, then alternately
tighten and loosen the grip — and watch what happens at the
front end, the muzzle of the gun. Later he or she can hold the
weapon pointed at some reference spot on a wall and watch
what happens when different fingers of the hand are used to
put major pressure on the grip or when it is gripped too tight.
The importance of sight alignment needs only to be docu-
mented by noting the short distance between the sights. An
individual does not have to be mechanically inclined to realize
a slight error in this short distance is going to be greatly mag-
nified over the longer distance the bullet has to travel to hit the

33

target. The word *aiming* implied direction toward an object and it is not too difficult to realize that unless a weapon is aimed at what the shooter hopes to hit, there is a little likelihood of accuracy, and it is almost equally simple to understand that the trigger pressure must be exerted in a manner that does not disturb aiming the weapon.

The correct grip, the manner in which the sights are aligned and aimed upon the target, and trigger pressure sum up the principles of pistol shooting. These are the things that must be learned before effective fire can be delivered at any target: bull's-eye, silhouette, or opponent.

While it is true that directing fire from the hip or shooting from any of the point-fire positions appears to imply only a need to "blast 'em off," it is equally true that all of these positions require directing fire — despite the fact that the sights are not utilized — and also require a standard method of gripping the weapon and correct trigger pressure.

A GOOD GRIP

A good grip is one that meets the requirements of holding the weapon in alignment on the target through the trigger pressure period and controlling the effect of the recoil sufficiently to permit rapid recovery. The correct grip is the one that is not only adjusted to these requirements but is also adapted to the hand of the individual shooter.

Most beginners seem to grip the gun incorrectly at the outset. The revolver or automatic pistol is not a baseball bat, and it is not grasped as one. The backstrap — the metal strip between the stocks on the rear of the gun — should be centered in the palm of the hand; then the lower three fingers are wrapped around the stocks as far as they can reach; the thumb is placed in a low position on the side of the frame of the revolver.

First, grasp the barrel of the weapon with the nonshooting hand and "fit" the gun into your shooting hand, moving the entire grip slightly to the right around the stocks as you do so. This is the correct grip, but it must be adapted to the individual hand.

Gripping the Revolver Correctly

Unlike automatic pistols,* the position of the revolver in the grip can be changed by moving it upward or downward or to the right or left. It should only be moved to the right when the shooter finds that he cannot conveniently manipulate either the hammer or the trigger.

In adjusting the hand to the proper grip, remember that the rear portion of the hand can be moved up or down without moving the front portion — the fingers. In single-action fire, the hammer must be cocked for each shot; therefore, it is easy to understand why the grip must be adjusted so that the thumb of the shooter can operate the hammer. Unless the grip is taken so that the center of the ball of the shooter's thumb actuates the hammer spur, a great deal of unnecessary twisting and turning of the gun is required to complete the cocking motion (Figs. 5 and 6).

In double-action fire, the crucial finger is the index finger as the hammer is cocked by pulling on the trigger. Some officers feel their fingers are too short for this type of fire, but a slight movement of the entire grip to the right (right-handed shooters) permits them to insert the index finger well into the trigger guard.

In combat shooting, it is desirable to adjust to a good double-action grip and then use the same grip whenever possible when shooting single action. Many "old hands" at formal target shooting may wish to use a "high-thumb" single-action grip, but new shooters should seek a grip suited to both types of fire, and it should be a grip that can be secured as the weapon is drawn from the holster.

Combat shooting problems of accuracy and control of the recoil of heavy weapons have led to the development of the two-hand grip. In shooting, the revolver is gripped first by the shooting hand, then the nonshooting hand grasps the fingers and base of the shooting hand in support (Fig. 7).

---

*See Chapter 6 for the directions on shooting combat automatic pistols.

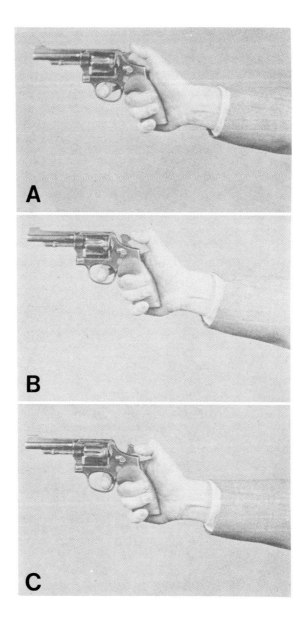

Figure 5. Cocking the Revolver in Single-Action Fire. (A) Thumb is placed on the hammer spur without loosening the three fingers that hold the weapon. (B and C) The hammer is cocked with a downward pressure of the thumb and without twisting or turning the muzzle of the revolver.

Figure 6. Grip for Single-Action Shooting. Author demonstrates correct grip for single-action shooting, a grip commonly used by police in target shooting at bull's-eye targets. Note that the thumb is higher than in the combat or double-action grip and that no more than the first joint of the trigger finger rests on the trigger. In other respects, there is little difference between the two grips.

Combat shooters should always be alert to the fact that the two-handed grip sometimes leads to a loosening of the gun hand grip upon the revolver or pistol. There must be a continuing vigilance to guard against any relaxing of the normal one-hand grip upon a handgun when the shooting hand is supported by the nonshooting hand.

Once the gun is fitted into the hand of the shooter, the question of pressure comes up. Shall pressure be applied in a "strangling" manner, choking the gun, or should pressure be applied at only certain points? It is obvious that the best points of pressure to hold the sights in alignment are the two semiflat

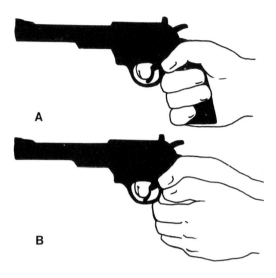

Figure 7. The Combat Grip — Revolvers. (A) The thumb of the shooting hand is locked in a low position, and the trigger finger is placed well into the trigger guard. Remaining fingers grasp the revolver with a constant and firm pressure. (B) In the two-handed grip, the major function of the nonshooting hand is to support the shooting hand and gun.

surfaces of either side of the grip. However, the human hand cannot exert equal pressure on these various surfaces, and such pressure at these points would not overcome the effect of the recoil. Therefore, the two points of pressure must be the front surface of the grip and the rear surface. The muscular pressure is exerted on the front of the grip against that portion of the hand that backs up the gun.

The thumb, its fatty base, and the palm of the hand are firm. The thumb should not exert real pressure on the gun. It is not relaxed, for it requires some rigidity to hold it in place. The best description is that it is *locked* in place.

The question of whether or not the pressure is applied equally with all fingers is best answered by looking at your fingers. The middle finger is the longest and naturally the strongest; the ring finger is next in length and strength; followed by the little finger. A natural exertion of pressure on the grip results in the middle finger doing most of the work and the little finger doing very little. If you have more than the average strength in the little finger, it may be necessary to relax it slightly. The middle and ring fingers should do all of the work, for pressure at the bottom of the grip causes trouble.

Pressure upon the grip must be constant; it cannot increase or decrease as the trigger is pressed to the rear. To hold the sights in alignment, the pressure must be constant; any tightening causes the sights to move out of alignment, just as any marked loosening of the grip does the same thing. "Freezing" on the trigger is a common fault, and the major cause is a tendency to tighten the pressure on the grip instead of increasing the pressure on the trigger.

Possibly the greatest fault in combat double-action shooting is "milking" the grip as the trigger pressure is applied. Sometimes this is an almost convulsive tightening of the entire hand — much as a farmer milks a cow — each time a shot is fired. Naturally, any accuracy possible from either a pointing or an aiming position is ruined by this movement which disturbs the natural pointing position of the gun or ruins the position of the aimed weapon.

The amount of pressure that should be exerted upon the grip is determined by several things; the most important of these is the condition of the muscles and the amount of practice and experience that the individual shooter has had in grasping the gun. The beginner cannot be expected to grip a gun as hard as one who has practiced a great deal, or as tight as one who has a well-developed grip through exercise.

The beginner should grip a gun just as hard as he or she can but not so hard that the revolver shakes because of muscular tension. Beginners should use an exerciser to build up their ability to grip the gun even harder. It is easy to see that the harder the grip the better the control, and with good control it is relatively simple to keep the weapon in alignment and prevent the gun from twisting or jumping in the hand due to the effect of the recoil.

A good grip is a precious thing. It should not be changed except for good reasons. The shooter who is constantly changing his grip finds that each change lessens the accuracy of his fire. Once a good grip is developed, the shooter should not make even minor changes in it unless absolutely necessary.

CORRECT COMBAT SIGHTING AND AIMING

In aligning the sights of a revolver or automatic pistol, the shooter places the body of the front sight in the center of the notch of the rear sight (Fig. 8A). The tops of both sights are level, and neither they nor the gun is canted to the right or left — downward. The correctly aligned sights are usually "picked up" by a shooter as he brings his or her weapon up into the line of sight to the target. A rough alignment of the sights is made anywhere on or near the target, then the gun is moved

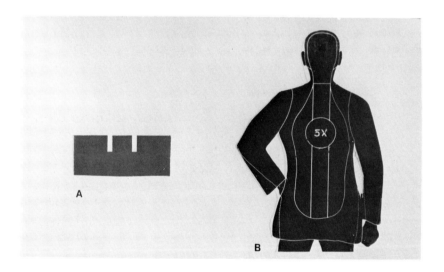

Figure 8. Correct Sight Picture. (A) The top of both sights are level, and the front sight is centered in the rear sight notch. (B) The 5-X ring on the silhouette target used for police combat practice is slightly above the center of the target. Hits in the 5-X ring earn the highest possible score. To achieve high scores, combat shooters should use the 5-X ring as the center of their aiming area, holding their *aligned sights* (A) in and around the 5-X ring. Some combat shooting instructors term this the *armpit hold*.

toward the center of the target as the shooter attempts to improve the alignment of the sights.

Combat firearms should be sighted-in to hit where aimed. Adjustable sights make this sighting-in a simple process of trial and error. If the gun involved has fixed sights, any adjustment may require a trip to a gunsmith. These sights may be filed for minor adjustments, but unless a shooter has some expertise in handling a file, it is better to seek the help of a gunsmith.

In combat shooting, the general area of aiming is the center of the mass of the target. In combat shooting on police ranges, the combat targets are man-sized outlines (silhouettes) printed in black. For scoring purposes, these targets have a centered five ring, and in mid-chest center a 5-X ring to indicate excellent shots. As a result, the aiming area in combat shooting on the police range is generally the chest area. Some instructors suggest holding the aligned sights at the center of the silhouette target at about the armpit level (Fig. 8B).

Look at the Sights

Where the eye or eyes should be focused seems to confuse many shooters. It is common knowledge that the eyes cannot be focused on two objects so far removed from each other as the sights and the aiming point without having faulty vision on one or the other. No one would try to read a newspaper held at arm's length at the same time that he was trying to read lettering on a sign 20 to 25 yards distant. No, he would read one or the other. He would say it was impossible to do both at the same time. But give the same person a gun and a target and he will try to look at — read — the sights at the same time that his eyes are focused on the target.

It is a physical impossibility to focus the eyes on both sights and target at the same time; one or the other is not brought into sharp relief. Therefore, the shooter must look *at* the sights by focusing directly upon them. The target does not have to be perfectly clear, but the sights must be outlined distinctly. It is the relation of the sights to each other that is all-important.

The relation of sights to target is secondary. It does not matter whether the hold is not perfect; if the sights are lined up, the bullet will strike where the sights are aimed. On the other hand, though the hold is excellent, a poor shot results if the sights are not lined up properly.

When the arm is extended, the initial sight alignment is usually good because the shooter is looking *at* the sights, but as he starts to aim the gun — to hold somewhere upon the target — then the trouble starts.

Most tyros have a decided tendency to focus the eyes upon the target, to concentrate on the relation of the front sight and the bull's-eye, and to keep the sights in alignment with each other only because they are in the field of vision. This is normal; every shooter has experienced it. The warning signal is "fuzzy" or "hairy" sights.

When the sights are first lined up, they are clear, sharply defined, but as the shooter continues to hold, the sight becomes fuzzy; the sharp picture of front and rear sights is not there. True, the target is sharply defined, but the sights are not. *Fuzzy, blurry,* or *hairy* sights are the signal that the eyes are being focused on the target, that the shooter is looking *through* the sights instead of *at* them.

This fact must be realized: A shooter cannot normally focus his eyes on the sights and the target at the same time, and it is more important to focus on the sights. Therefore, it would seem that every shooter could readily line up his sights and keep them in alignment once he realized this fact, but while many individuals know it to be a fact, only a small number seem to have the ability to remember it. This is particularly strange when we are also aware of the fact that the sights "fuzz" up when we are looking through them instead of at them.

Excellent shooting coaches sometimes insist on a shooter "talking to himself" as he shoots. They advise the use of these subvocal messages as a device to keep the importance of looking at the sights within the conscious thinking of the shooter at the all-important time of aiming his weapon.

AREA AIMING

Area aiming is a theory of handgun shooting directly opposed to the point-of-aim school of thought.

Area aiming is based on the fact that it is difficult to hold a revolver on any certain "point" on a target. An aiming point is in reality an aiming area. Perhaps the fault lies with aiming charts. These charts show the sights of a gun faultlessly aimed at a point just below the bull's-eye. Perhaps it lies with shooters who stress the fact that they show a "line of white" at the bottom of the bull's-eye, or others who say they hold on the "neck" of combat targets.

It is almost a physical impossibility for any person to hold a gun steady. Actually, shooters try to hold as close as they can to their imagined point and thus confine the natural movement of their gun to a limited area with such point in the center of that area. This is simple enough for experienced shooters, but it has bewildered beginners for many years. The experienced shooter explains to a novice shooter just where to hold, but fails to explain that anywhere close to that point was the best that could be expected.

Every shooter's arm shakes or moves when he is aiming a gun, but the extent of the movement depends on muscles and nerves. The experienced shooter's muscles and nerves are conditioned and trained; his natural movement is much less, and his aiming area is thereby cut down. He may think he is holding on an aiming point because he does not move too far away from it, but move he does, whether he realizes it or not (Fig. 9).

The belief that you must hold on an aiming point is harmful to the new shooter; he will try to do something that is *just not possible*. It has also harmed even veteran shooters. It is this belief that causes a shooter to try to "frame" a shot — to make the gun go off when it is aimed exactly at the aiming point. Naturally, the effort to make the gun go off results in a sudden pressure on the trigger. This "jerking" of the trigger also leads to "flinching." Either fault can be ruinous. When the handgunner puts any sudden pressure on the trigger to make his pistol or revolver go off, he also disturbs his aim, just at the

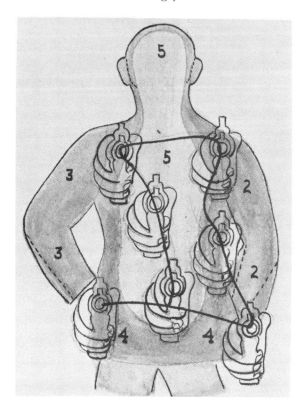

Figure 9. Area Aiming. Every shooter wavers to some degree. This schematic drawing represents the actual movement pattern of a new shooter. Area aiming is based upon this waver pattern. The shooter maintains trigger pressure as his weapon moves around on the target, and when the shot goes off, it usually hits somewhere within the waver area. However, the shooter who fights this elementary rule and puts a sudden pressure on the trigger at the moment of precisely perfect sighting at some point on the target discovers that the shot does not hit this point and frequently does not even hit the target. This sudden pressure is *jerking* and leads to an almost involuntary muscular reaction to meet the recoil, known as *flinching*. Either one ruins accuracy.

critical moment prior to the ignition of the cartridge. He "jerks" the shot low and left. This disturbance of a shooter's aim may be further complicated by the normal human reaction to the knowledge that a handgun is about to go off with its resultant noise and recoil — "flinching." That reaction is a lunging forward to meet the expected recoil; the heeling of the gun to produce a hit high and right.

A novice shooter should realize that he cannot hold a gun steady but that he or she can hold it steady enough to confine the movement of his sights to an area. In the beginning, a novice can hold well within a 10- to 12-inch circle at 25 yards. If he aligns his sights properly, presses on the trigger in such a manner that the letoff is good, and aims within such a circle, all his shots will hit in that area. Since that area is equal to the "kill" area on the silhouette target or the area of the eight ring of a bull's-eye target, he should shoot a fair score.

REVOLVER TRIGGER PRESSURE

Trigger pressure for single-action shooting of a revolver starts by placing some portion of the first joint of the index finger upon the trigger. Many good shooters claim that the extreme tip of the finger should be used, but this depends on each individual shooter, the length of his fingers, his grip, and what is even more important — what feels most natural to the individual concerned. When a shooter has secured his grip, he should place on the trigger that portion of the first joint of his index finger which seems to give him the best control. That is the correct finger position *for him.* To bend the trigger finger into an unnatural position because some expert shoots with the tip of his finger or because some book once stated that good trigger control could only be secured in such and such a fashion is downright ridiculous.

In double-action revolver shooting, it is necessary to put the finger further into the trigger guard than in single-action fire, in order to secure a good "bite" on the trigger for the much heavier double-action trigger pull. However, several excellent shooters fire double action with only the tip of their finger on the trigger — proving that despite the type of shooting, every person must develop a "custom" finger position that provides effective trigger control.

Pressure on the trigger is directly to the rear along the same line as the barrel axis. Some old rifle shooters may have a tendency to press downward; shooters using the second joint of their finger have a tendency to pull the trigger to the right;

shooters who squeeze with the extreme tip of their finger seem
to have a slight tendency to press to the left. Any pressure other
than straight to the rear is transmitted to the entire revolver
when the hammer is released and usually disturbs the sight
alignment between the time of the hammer release and the
actual ignition of the cartridge. Make every effort not to let any
such tendency become a habit.

A pressure on the trigger other than to the rear can be de-
tected by lining up the sights, putting almost enough pressure
on the trigger to set it off — but not quite enough — carefully
watching the sights, and then releasing the pressure entirely. If
you have been pressing the trigger downward or to the side, the
front sight moves in the direction of the released pressure. If the
trigger is being pressed straight to the rear and the above test is
made, the sights do not move out of alignment.

The easiest way to assure pressure directly to the rear is to
pick a spot on the inner surface of your hand directly behind
the trigger and then try to press toward such spot with that
portion of your finger that rests upon the trigger.

Picking such a spot and pressing toward it every time you
press on the trigger also helps to overcome a natural desire to
tighten up on the grip with the other fingers as pressure is
placed upon the trigger. This tendency must be guarded
against, for any increase in pressure on the grip ruins your
alignment and also the control of the pressure on the trigger.

A shooter can put the proper pressure on the trigger all day
when he knows the gun is empty, but when it is fired a few
times, the desire to excel takes over. In such cases, unless area
aiming has become habituated, an attempt will be made to
frame the shot and jerk the trigger when the shooter wants the
gun to go off. Then, after a few belts from the recoil of a heavy-
caliber gun, it is only normal to punch forward to meet
the recoil when an individual knows the weapon is about to
go off.

The two-stage, double-action trigger motion (Fig. 10) enables
some revolver shooters to achieve better trigger control. By
breaking up the double-action trigger motion into two stages,
the shooter is, in effect, cocking the hammer in the first stage

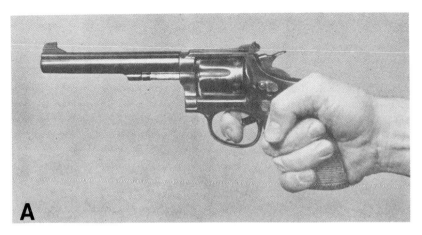

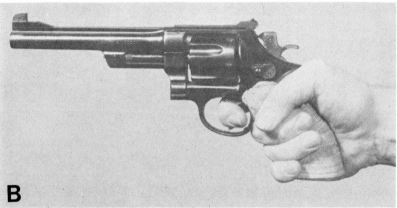

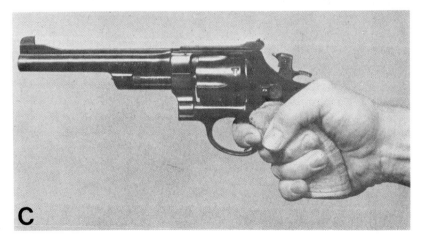

Figure 10. The Two-Stage Double-Action Trigger Pull. (A) Trigger finger starts the trigger moving to the rear with a strong, rapid movement. (B) Trigger finger moves fast, and the hammer starts through its cocking motion. (C) Rapid, rearward motion of the trigger finger is braked by the contact of the tip of the trigger finger with a pressure point. Note the hammer position: It is almost ready to fall forward.

and then squeezing off the trigger in the second stage. In this two-stage trigger motion, the shooter should rapidly take up the heavy trigger pressure in the first stage, turning the cylinder with this rapid and firm motion; then the heavy trigger pull is squelched during the second stage so that, at the moment of hammer release, there is no jarring stop of the trigger finger to move the aimed revolver away from the aiming area.

Some shooters achieve total trigger finger control, and they can move through the two-stage pull without using a "pressure point." In using a pressure point, a shooter positions his grip and trigger-finger position so that, at the end of the first stage of the double-action trigger motion, the tip of the trigger finger strikes the rear of the trigger guard or the projection of a custom grip at this point. It is this contact with the pressure point that alerts the shooter to the fact he has concluded the first stage of this motion and must ease off into the second stage.

Many inexperienced shooters assume that the trigger can be swept through its motion in any manner because they are attempting something called combat or "practical" pistol shooting on a range. Nothing could be further from the truth or prepare them less for actual delivery of accurate fire in combat situations.

A trigger can be pressed through its motion very rapidly — either in single- or double-action fire — but it must be actuated in such a manner that the aim or "pointing" of the weapon is not disturbed if the shooter wishes to hit the target at which he has been aiming or pointing his gun.

COMBAT LOADING THE REVOLVER

Once a police officer has emptied his revolver in armed combat, he is confronted with the problem of reloading his revolver as fast as possible. First, it must be rapidly unloaded, then quickly reloaded.

To unload, the following procedure is suggested: The officer should reach forward with his or her weak hand, palm up and open, at the same time shift the thumb on the gun slightly to actuate the cylinder latch, and drop the gun into the palm of the weak hand. (Practice at this maneuver makes it possible to utilize the coming together of the gun and the palm of the hand to open the cylinder.) As the cylinder swings open, the shooter places the thumb of his weak hand on the ejector rod, curls his remaining fingers around the open cylinder and frame of the gun, and ejects the fired cases.

With the muzzle of the weapon down slightly, but with the gun's position not changed too much, the new ammunition is quickly placed in the chambers of the revolver. To facilitate loading, the thumb of the weak hand is moved from the tip of the ejector rod (after ejecting the empty shells) to the side of the cylinder. In this position, it assists the middle finger of the same hand in rotating the cylinder as each chamber is loaded. Placing the weapon in the palm of the hand as it is loaded is excellent protection against loss of time due to dropping cartridges on the ground (Fig. 11).

Speed-loading devices for quickly placing six cartridges in the cylinder of a revolver has made the method of "stuffing" cartridges by hand into the cylinder one-by-one obsolete under combat or combat-training conditions (Fig. 11B and C). Belt pouches are available that make these loading devices readily available within the reach of the officer's free hand.

Combat unloading is now attempted with one hand, dumping the shells out. Unfortunately, after firing, empty cartridge cases often have a tendency to resist total ejection, hanging three quarters of the way out and requiring the use of the officer's hand to pick them out.

Once the revolver is free of empty shells, the speed-loading device with its six fresh cartridges is taken from the belt and the tips of the cartridges are slipped into the chambers of the cylinder. A simple tug or twist of the hand results in the release of the six fresh cartridges. Usually, they drop into position, but sometimes one or two of them may require a push to seat them completely and allow the cylinder of the revolver to be closed. Despite minor faults, these speed reloaders are a tremendous improvement over loading cartridges one at a time.

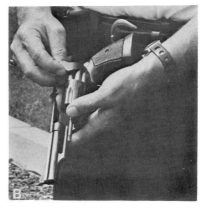

Figure 11. (A) Combat Loading Position. The gun is cradled in the hand of the shooter, the thumb and middle fingers of the hand steady and turn the cylinder as each chamber is loaded, and the palm of the hand serves as a tray to catch any cartridge which the shooter might fumble and drop. This technique is excellent for loading at night, as the palm of the hand serves both as a rest and a guide to the cylinder. (B and C) Speed-Loading Devices. (B) Six cartridges are inserted into the revolver's cylinder with a pull on the speed-loading device. Pictured is the RL Series Revolver Loader®, manufactured by Kubik Products, Inc., of a specially formulated plastic resin reinforced with glass. (C) The Six-Second Revolver Reloader®, manufactured by the H.K.S. Tool Products Company. This device is part aluminum and part high-impact plastic. It operates by turning of the knurled knob.

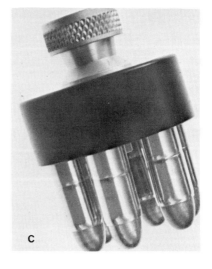

Conclusion

Possibly the key to the basic principles of combat shooting rests with area aiming. It is the attempt to be too precise in shooting with a pistol or revolver that leads to gross inaccuracies or to complete misses. It may be that this weapon was never intended to be shot with as much preciseness as a rifle. Shooting the pistol is one instance in which an excess of precision can defeat your purpose — the attempt to deliver accurate fire.

No step in this basic phase of shooting can be excluded from the learning program; each must be learned and then integrated into the job of shooting. As a coach, I usually sum it up in these words: "Just line up the sights with each other and put a slow, steady pressure on the trigger. As long as you see any part of that target in front of your sights, keep up the trigger pressure, adding to it as your gun comes toward the middle of your target . . . and as you fight to keep the sights lined up."

Determination is a valuable trait at this stage of learning to shoot a pistol or revolver: determination to line up the sights with each other, to aim in an area rather than at any point on the target, and to place the correct pressure on the trigger.

Chapter 5

AIMED FIRE

AIMED fire is more concerned with the classic principles of shooting than is directed fire, particularly in the areas of looking at the sights and aiming. However, since the target of police gunfire is the criminal who lives by no "sporting" or gentlemen's code, the classic off-hand shooting position has been junked. The jungle or gutter code of the armed criminal supports shooting without warning or provocation. The police officer must take a position that provides some protection and improves his ability to deliver effective fire.

In combat shooting, it is basic instruction to advise shooters that both eyes must be open when the sights are lined up and the weapon aimed at the target. If an officer closes one eye, he blinds himself to any accomplice of his opponent who might move into the combat on the side of the closed eye. Make your own test: Open both eyes, look straight ahead, and notice the periphery of your vision; it extends in at least a 180° arc. You may not be able to read signs to your own immediate right or left, but you notice movement. Now close one eye and note the diminishing of your field of view — it is reduced by at least 40 percent.

There should be little need to speak about trigger pressure in combat shooting, as police officers should graduate to combat shooting only after proving proficiency at ordinary bull's-eye targets. Officers should at least be certain they have arrived at the plateau of knowledge at which they can recognize their own *modus operandi* when they jerk the trigger or flinch to meet the recoil.

The accuracy of aimed fire on silhouette targets representing an opponent is based on effective use of the sights on the revolver and the ability to aim and fire without putting a sudden pressure on the trigger — disturbing the sight alignment and aim at the moment of cartridge ignition. Normal accuracy is improved by taking positions that take advantage of every possible support: barricades, cars, trees, fences, and the ground itself.

In aimed-fire positions, the weapon is held at the end of an extended arm, with the revolver as far as possible from the eyes. The sights on a revolver are scaled to normal shooting at arm's length and the shooter fires with more of a "rough" sight the closer he brings them to his eyes. Another factor which may only change the point of impact slightly, but possibly means a "miss" at times, is the fact that the normal grip and recoil platform for the gun is usually at the end of an extended arm, and as the arm is bent and brought closer to the eye, a slight change occurs. This is not a factor in directed fire, as the gun is zeroed in with the line of sight through muscular coordination, but when an officer is shooting aimed fire with a gun sighted in for a normal position, and he varies his position, it is likely he will have changes in the point of impact. Changing positions may only take a minute, but why throw away accuracy?

In any aimed-fire position, the head is held as erect as possible so that the shooter's vision is not obscured by his upper eyelashes. This is difficult with a low prone position, and it is wise to bring the gun to a higher position, if the sights "fuzz up," so that the head may be raised for better vision. In sitting, kneeling, and standing positions, the head should always be held erect, the gaze directed at the target, and the gun and sights brought up into the line of sight.

WEAK-HAND SHOOTING

In the more rapid phases of police combat shooting at short ranges, speed of getting into effective action was a defense against enemy fire. For that reason, the discussion of shooting with the weak hand was placed in this chapter on more deliberate aimed fire. The strong hand is the one normally used in shooting.

It must be remembered, though, that a disabling wound can occur at any time, and if time is available, a police officer should fire with his weak hand at every stage of combat shooting in order to gain experience and skill. Accuracy of fire, when the strong hand has been disabled and when an opponent might be moving in close for the kill, is certainly highly desirable. Practice is the only sure way of acquiring the necessary skill.

The grip with the weak hand is the same as with the strong hand, and the basic principles of sights, aim, and trigger letoff also remain the same — and have equal importance in achieving accuracy.

The need for shooting with the weak as well as the strong hand of a police officer is slowly driving the fancy grips out of police holsters and off the ranges used for practical course firing. A generous thumbrest might be very desirable for single-action target shooting or even some form of combat shooting, such as aimed fire stages, but it is certainly a handicap when the hand holding the gun is changed, and the thumbrest makes it difficult or almost impossible for the trigger finger to reach into the trigger guard and secure adequate trigger control.

THE PRONE POSITION

In the prone position, the shooter not only presents a very small target, but also utilizes the best possible support for his firearm — the ground. The body of the shooter is positioned directly behind the weapon, with the feet together, unlike the rifleman's prone position, in which the body rests at a 45° angle to the line of fire and the feet are spread wide apart. The gun itself is not permitted to touch the ground; the shooter's free hand is utilized as a support between the ground and the gun. The ideal position is one in which the flat portion of both forearms are rested upon the ground, with the gun butt and the hand grasping the weapon resting in the palm of the free hand, and the back of the free hand resting upon the ground. However, high grass sometimes does not permit this position, and it is necessary for the shooter to sometimes make a fist of his free hand and rest it upon the ground to support his gun and the hand holding it (Fig. 12).

Figure 12. The position of the shooter's hand in the prone position must allow a clear view of sights and the target. Head is as erect as possible, the weapon is as far away from the eyes as an extended arm permits, and the body is fully extended in a position of rest. Note how the nonshooting hand, resting directly on the ground, supports the base of the shooting hand and the butt of the revolver. The entire bone structure of the body is relaxed and resting upon the ground — a position of great stability.

Police officers should keep this position in mind, even in room-sized shooting situations. The records of two or three gunfights in recent years revealed the officer had dropped to the floor and delivered his fatal fire from a prone position.

In firing the various combat courses, it is required that the shooter drops to his knees, draws his revolver, assumes the prone position, and opens fire. In actual combat, the officer might drop and roll as he drew his weapon — movement is always desirable when an opponent is shooting, and it minimizes the criminal's ability to score hits.

Figure 13. (A) The High Kneeling Position. Two views show the straight back and unsupported two-hand grip used in this position. Foot and knee placement offers the shooter a firm foundation and some assurance against the body sway. This is an excellent combat position, as a shooter can drop into it quickly and it offers good target reduction, as opposed to the standing position. (B) The Kneeling Position. The shooter sits on his right heel, flexing the toes of his right foot, and points his left toe toward the target. The left arm is well down on the forward knee to rest on the flat of the upper arm for greater support. Some shooters extend the shooting arm fully forward and support this arm just back of the wrist with the nonshooting hand. (C) The major bones of the body provide an almost trusslike support for the gun in the kneeling positions. Note how the upper portion of the body is supported by the bent left leg of the shooter and how the right leg braces the entire body for stability.

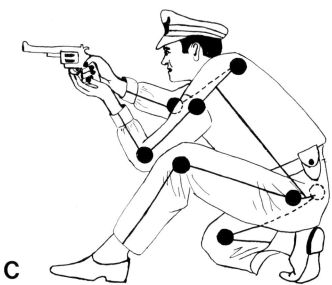

Figure 13. (B and C).

THE KNEELING POSITION

The kneeling position, in which the free hand is used to support the shooting hand, has two variations: the high position for very rapid aimed fire and the normal kneeling position (Fig. 13). The low or normal position requires time to assume but also provides much greater support than is possible in the high position.

The high position provides no support for the arms of the shooter. On the other hand the normal position provides good support. In this position, the gun arm is supported between wrist and elbow by the free arm as it rests upon the forward knee of the shooter. The steadiness of this position rests on the fact that the extended gun arm receives a trusslike support from the other arm as the inside, flat surface of the biceps area of this arm is supported upon the knee (Fig. 13).

In all kneeling positions, the forward foot is pointed toward the target. The rear foot is placed far to the rear in the low position for more effective balance, but it is tucked under the body in the normal or high position. In the normal position, some shooters sit on the heel of the rear foot, flexing the foot and resting upon the bent toes; others prefer a slightly lower position secured by turning the foot slightly and sitting on it.

THE SITTING POSITION

As it is close to the ground, with both arms supporting the weapon, the sitting position is one of the best positions for effective combat fire. The shooter can draw his revolver as he drops into position and have it in action almost before his buttocks stop bouncing from the impact with the ground. It is excellent for shooting from behind the protection of low walls, buildings, and breaks in the ground.

In the sitting position, the toes of both feet point toward the target and are fairly close together (Fig. 14). The knees are spread slightly to support the flat portion of each elbow, while the free hand supports the hand holding the weapon at the base

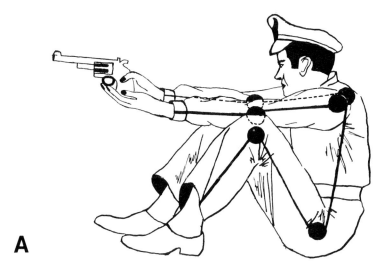

A

B

Figure 14. Sitting Positions. (A) The Basic Sitting Position. The weight distribution of the shooter's body is centered. In this position, each shooter must find the point of rest for his forearms that gives his gun arm the greatest support and the entire position a feeling of stability as the weapon is fired. The elbow joints should not be any further forward than shown in this sketch nor the knee joints any higher in relation to the junction of the elbow. Note the stability of this position: Both feet are planted firmly on the ground, the bone structure of the legs supports the arms, and both of the hands merge into a common and well-supported grip on the weapon. (B) The California Sitting Position. The gun arm is rested on the right knee, between the wrist and elbow, with improved stability as the point of rest moves toward the gun. Both buttocks are the base of the trusslike support of the bent leg, and the entire body is further steadied by the free hand of the shooter. This is an amazing position of rest and one that may be dropped into with little effort.

of the gun. In this position, the shooter adjusts for major changes in elevation by moving both feet forward or to the rear, thus depressing or raising his knee level, which, in turn, brings about the desired vertical correction by lowering or raising both arms. This is vital to top accuracy in this position, as any pronounced bending of the wrist from a natural position means slower recovery of aim between shots — the wrist has to be readjusted after each shot, as it returns to its natural position. It is also important that the gun is brought up to eye level, rather than the eye down to gun level.

Variations of the sitting position that require a "squeezing" pressure by the legs or thighs of a shooter to steady the aim or adjust for elevation tend to lower the accuracy potential of this fine position by making muscular tension a factor, rather than depending on the bone structure of the body for support.

In the California sitting position, the shooter drops to the ground in a sitting position, but only one knee is raised to support the shooting hand. The other leg is stretched out full length, and the nonshooting hand is placed flat against the ground to the rear to "prop" the officer's leaning-back position (Fig. 14B).

BARRICADE SHOOTING

In shooting from behind a protective wall, the side of a building, or other barricade, the police officer seeks both protection and a support for his weapon.

Dramatic reduction of target area can be secured by shooting from the protection of a wall or the corner of a building. As simulated in the barricade shooting of the Practical Pistol Course, there is a reduction of 90 percent in the target area offered for enemy fire — only the side of the shooter's face, his shoulder, and his gun arm project beyond the barricade. Support is very effective, because in barricade shooting the weapon is almost as steady as the barricade itself.

In shooting from a position of rest, the officer must be careful that no portion of the weapon is permitted to rest directly on any barricade or other support. The weapon must be cushioned in some fashion or it may be damaged in recoil. In combat shooting, it is usually cushioned with the free hand. It must also be realized that the muzzle of the firearm must be free of any obstruction of the barricade and clear of the supporting fingers of the free hand, or the shooter will be picking wood splinters, brick dust, or particles of lead out of his head and possibly whistling for first aid through a neat hole in one of his fingers.

In shooting from behind a barricade simulating the side of a building or the edge of a doorway, the shooter places his feet in what appears to be an unbalanced position in order to secure as much protection of the barricade as possible. In shooting with the right hand, the *left* foot is forward, and in shooting on the other side of a barricade with the left hand, the *right* foot is forward.

The most common method of supporting a revolver in barricade shooting is to place the palm and extended fingers of the free hand flat against the barricade with the extended fingers up and the thumb spread out just beyond the edge of the barricade, thus forming a *V* into which the shooter places the wrist of his gun hand (Fig. 15B).

Placing the flat underside of the free-hand wrist against the barricade at its edge is an additional method. The shooting hand and weapon is then extended beyond the edge of the barricade, and the wrist of the shooting hand is grasped and steadied by the fingers of the free hand (Fig. 15C).

This is an excellent position, as the grasping of the shooting arm's wrist with the finger of the free hand not only provides a better support than the *V* normally used but also helps to speed up recovery of aim as it retards recoil.

The greatest error in taking barricade positions is the tendency to lean into the support too much. This usually occurs when the shooter places his feet too far from the barricade and is forced to bend into a half-crouch as he supports his hand. The ideal position is a standing position, with the weapon being brought up to eye level as the hands are placed against the barricade.

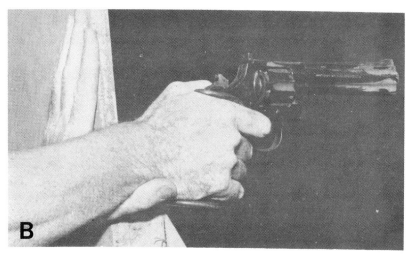

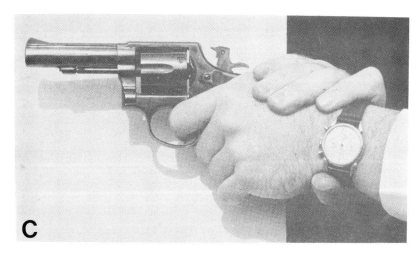

Conclusion

The modern police officer throws out the rules of pistol shooting as a sport in order to compete on more equal terms with the criminal likely to fight police. In every position of aimed fire in combat shooting, the gun is supported in some fashion, and in every position, the officer seeks to reduce the target area into which the criminal can place effective fire.

Shooting with one arm extended, with the free hand at the shooter's side, and making no contact with the firing-line bench or other support is strictly for target shooters.

It pleases me to see a policeman drop into a prone position and use the ground to support his shooting arm. All the criminal has to shoot at is a "looking-down" silhouette of head and shoulders — equal to about 15 percent of the standing position target area — and the cop has a firm base from which to direct his fire.

I like the ease with which the prone, sitting, and kneeling positions can be taken; I think barricade shooting teaches the utmost in concealment and reduction of target area.

Figure 15. Barricade Position. (A) The upright two-by-fours represent the barricade. The shooter on the left is right-handed and shooting with his strong hand. Note that his left foot is forward and that his left hand rests flat against the barricade. The shooter on the right is also right-handed but is firing with his weak hand. His right foot is forward, and the flat of his right hand is resting on the barricade. Both shooters are well positioned: close to the barricade, leaning into it slightly, and with heads erect. This position supports the gun hand with the extended thumb of the hand resting flat against the barricade. (B) The nonshooting hand is placed against the barricade. It is flattened so that the entire inner surface of the hand, from the tips of the fingers to the heel of the palm, rests firmly against the barricade. Thus supported, the thumb of the shooter provides a shelf upon which to rest the wrist of the gun-holding arm. (C) A new method of barricade shooting. The fingers of the nonshooting hand are clasped around the shooter's wrist while the base of the hand rests against the barricade and supports the shooting hand in a remarkably steady position.

Chapter 6

SHOOTING COMBAT
AUTOMATIC PISTOLS

S HOOTING the combat automatic pistol requires the same firm and constant grip as in shooting the
revolver, equal or greater care in aligning the sights and
aiming, and a smooth trigger letoff.

Automatic pistol shooters use the same combat positions as
revolver shooters. The rules for position shooting apply
equally to shooters using revolvers and automatic pistols,
whether in directed fire from the hip or shoulder or aimed fire
from the standing, kneeling, sitting, or prone positions.

GRIPPING THE AUTOMATIC PISTOL

The combat automatic pistol should be positioned in the
palm of the shooting hand so that the heavy recoil common to
9 mm and .45 caliber handguns is cushioned by the hand and
arm of the shooter. A position of the grip quite comfortable for
most shooters can be achieved by placing the automatic in the
V between the thumb and index finger of the shooting hand.
The thumb rests firmly against the receiver of the pistol and is
carried high or at least level with the index finger, rather than
being clamped in a downward position, as in combat revolver
shooting. Some portion of the index finger's first joint is placed
on the trigger, and the remaining fingers of the shooting hand
are placed around the main portion of the grip. The pressure of
these fingers is exerted to the rear against the palm of the
shooter's hand. Figures 16 and 17 illustrate the correct method
of gripping the combat automatic pistol. Ideally, the major
grip pressure is exerted by the middle finger of the shooter's
hand, then — in diminishing order — by the ring and little
fingers.

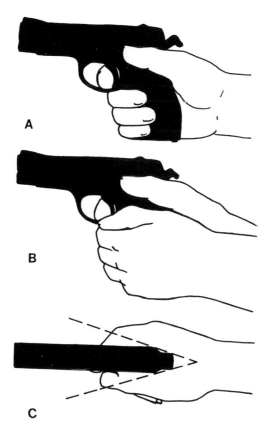

Figure 16. The Combat Grip — Automatic Pistols. (A) In grasping the automatic pistol for combat firing, the thumb of the shooting hand is extended along the grip, the tip or other portion of the first joint of the index finger is placed on the trigger, and the remaining fingers grasp the pistol with a firm and constant pressure. (B) In the two-handed grip, the fingers of the nonshooting hand support the shooting hand and the pistol. (C) Automatic pistols should be positioned in the shooter's hand in the **V** between the index finger and thumb.

Common faults in gripping the automatic pistol are listed:

1. The gun is positioned so that the thumb of the shooting hand rather than the palm takes the recoil shock.
2. The thumb of the shooter's hand exerts too little or too much pressure. A "floating" thumb (no pressure) is probably better than pressure that tends to push bullet impact

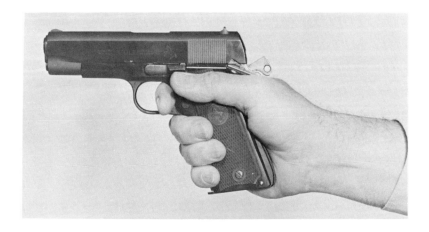

Figure 17. Side View of **V**-Positioned Grip. Centering the combat automatic pistol in the center of the **V** between the index finger and thumb of the shooting hand insures a *wraparound* grip that can be maintained shot after shot, despite the heavy recoil of 9 mm and .45 caliber cartridges. Note how the palm of the shooter's hand covers most of the backstrap of the pistol and the fatty portion of the thumb is in a position to hold the gun firmly and transfer the shock of recoil to the shooter's arm and body. (The gun shown is a Colt Commander in .45 ACP caliber.)

away from the aiming area. Trial and error indicates to each shooter the amount of pressure contributing to accuracy.

3. Placing the trigger finger inside of the trigger guard beyond the first joint: It is true that some shooters can shoot accurately with this placement of their trigger finger, but the first-joint placement is a comfortable position for effective trigger control.

4. Too much pressure with the little finger of the shooter's hand: This pressure at the bottom of the grip tends to push shots downward and away from the aiming area at the moment of firing. Since such pressure is usually accompanied by a lessening of the pressure of the middle finger, there is a general loosening of the entire grip that allows the sights to move out of alignment with each other and destroys the sight "picture" vital to accuracy.

Most shooters have a tendency to grip the combat automatic pistol incorrectly when they first fire it. Positioning the weapon in the *V* between the index finger and the thumb of the shooting hand is the first step in "fitting" the gun to the hand for the correct grip. If the shooter finds this position awkward, the gun can be shifted slightly toward the shooter's thumb. If an unpleasant recoil is felt by the thumb when firing, then the grip has been shifted too much. The best method is to cover the backstrap of the weapon with the palm of the hand as much as possible, utilizing the fatty base of the thumb as an integral portion of the grip.

The concept of a viselike grip[1] has been of help to many shooters seeking the correct grip for the combat automatic pistols. In the viselike grip, the two points of pressure are the front and rear surfaces of the grip (backstrap). Muscular pressure is exerted on the front of the grip against that portion of the hand that backs up the automatic pistol. The inner surfaces of the palm of the shooting hand covering the weapon's backstrap act as the stationary jaw of the vise and that portion of the shooter's fingers resting on the *front* of the grip as the moving jaw of the vise. As the grip pressure is exerted, it is similar to the moving jaw closing in and holding the gun against the stationary jaw of an imaginary vise.

THE SIGHT PICTURE

The correct sight picture for any handgun is developed by lining up the two sights: front and rear.

The importance of correct sight alignment is a key to accuracy with any handgun, but it is particularly important because most combat automatic pistols have a short sight radius. If the combat automatic pistol's sights are not correctly aligned with each other, the amount of error in the sight picture is much greater than if the sight radius had been longer, as with a revolver with a 6-inch barrel. For instance, the sight radius on the Colt Commander® automatic pistol is 5 3/4 inches as opposed to a sight radius of 7 5/8 inches on a Colt Python® revolver with a 6-inch barrel.

Many combat shooters find that it is easier to focus on the sights of a combat automatic pistol because of this short sight radius. There appears to be less tendency to focus on the front sight and to neglect the rear sight's appearance. Therefore, a shooter can overcome the handicap of a short sight radius on combat automatic pistols by concentrating on the alignment of the two sights.

I believe there is a need for great concentration upon looking *at* the sights of combat automatic pistols to bring them into sharp relief so that the front sight and the rear sight's notch and the tops of both of them are outlined distinctly against the target. Correct sight alignment means that the front sight is centered in the rear-sight notch, with the top of the front sight level with the top of the rear sight notch and the top of both sights level — that is, not "canted" to the right or left.

There is a linkup between sight alignment and the muscles controlling the wrist of the shooting hand. Once the shooter has taken the correct grip on an automatic pistol, there is no change in grip pressure to correct sight alignment; errors are corrected by slight movements of the wrist. Once corrected, the wrist is locked into position and the weapon and arm moved into the aiming area.

TRIGGER LETOFF

The manner in which the trigger is pressed to the rear to release the hammer on combat automatic pistols is very similar to the trigger pressure used in shooting revolvers single action. Unlike the double-action trigger motion of a revolver, there is no perceptible motion when pressing the trigger of a combat automatic pistol, and the trigger "pull" requires much less pressure to actuate than any double-action revolver trigger motion.

Many of the combat automatic pistols now have a "double-action" trigger capability, but it was never intended that the pistol be fired shot after shot with this double-action trigger pull. Originally, the design intent was to give a police officer a second chance at a cartridge that misfired. One of the classic arguments against the automatic pistol and in favor of the revolver was that the revolver readily presented a fresh cartridge to be fired in the event of a misfire, while automatic pistols had to be "charged" manually by the shooter — working the slide back and releasing it to place a new cartridge in firing position. The double-action capability of the new combat automatic pistols partially overcame this argument, as this feature does allow the shooter to quickly manipulate the trigger in a second attempt to fire a cartridge that failed to fire. Of course, when the cartridge does not fire on this second attempt, then the slide of the pistol must be moved back manually and released to put a fresh cartridge in firing position.

The double-action capability of combat automatic pistols has been recognized as a possible safety feature when a shooter does not wish to carry the weapon cocked and locked. In such event, the first shot is fired double action. However, it is grossly unfair to the fine combat automatic pistols having this double-action capability to suggest that a police officer must learn two trigger pulls when shooting them. The first is a double-action trigger procedure with considerable perceptible motion and pressure; the other is the standard trigger motion common to any automatic pistol in which the firing of one cartridge cocks the hammer of the weapon automatically (self-loading).

A police officer carrying a combat automatic pistol with the hammer down and a live cartridge in the chamber can fire the first shot double action with the same grip he or she would use in firing the remaining cartridges using the standard trigger motion. There is no need for any shifting of the combat grip in the transition from double action to standard trigger motion. In fact, it is important that police officers learn to fire these weapons using the same grip. In the event of a misfire, any time lost in shifting grips is disastrous in combat-shooting situations.

I have fired several thousand rounds from the Model 39 and Model 59 Smith and Wesson automatic pistols, switching from the standard trigger pressure to double action (simulating a misfire) and found I can hold the sights in alignment throughout the lengthy double-action trigger motion and keep the shot within the same group as shots fired with the standard trigger pressure. I found I could develop the correct motion by dry-practice firing with the empty gun while I kept the sights in alignment through *both* the rearward motion of the trigger and its forward motion.

At one time, I considered a double-action shot recovering from a misfire in a combat automatic pistol a "throw-away" to get the weapon into regular action again. This is no longer true.

A common characteristic of combat automatic pistols is "slack" in the standard trigger motion. This is the free motion before the trigger actually moves into its operation of releasing the hammer. The length of slack varies from gun to gun, but regardless of this variation, it is relatively easy to learn to take up the slack with a single firm motion before the steadily increasing trigger pressure is placed upon the trigger. Some combat shooters are annoyed at trigger slack and seek out a local gunsmith to remove it. This is not a difficult task for a competent gunsmith, but is unnecessary unless the individual shooter finds that the slack in his gun interferes with the correct trigger letoff.

The correct trigger letoff in shooting combat automatic pistols involves a steadily increasing pressure on the trigger while the aligned sights of the weapon are held in the aiming area. The word *letoff* in this connection implies that no sudden trigger pressure is made at the last instant.

The recommended steadily increasing pressure is just that. It is *not* a stop-and-go motion in which the shooter attempts to make the weapon fire when he or she wants it to fire. Shots can be fired rapidly with a steadily increasing trigger pressure without a sudden jerk of the trigger at the last moment before firing.

Trigger pressure starts by placing the tip or some other portion of the first joint of the index finger of the shooting hand upon the trigger. The exact position should be the one that gives a shooter the best feeling about trigger control and allows for pressure straight to the rear toward the palm of the shooter's hand, along the same line as the axis of the barrel.

Any pressure other than straight to the rear may be transmitted to the entire weapon at the moment of firing and can disturb the sight alignment during the split second between the time of hammer release and the actual ignition of the cartridge.

The concept of a steadily increasing trigger pressure when shooting combat automatic pistols does not mean that shots should be fired when the weapon's sights are not correctly aligned and the aligned sights not aimed within the shooter's aiming area. In mastering this trigger pressure, shooters must coordinate the rate of speed with which they put pressure upon the trigger with their ability to get the correct sight picture and hold it in their aiming area until the shot is fired. If the hold is not "good", the shooter should come back to a position of rest rather than firing the shot. After a sufficient amount of practice, shots can be fired while the sights are properly aligned and aimed somewhere in the shooter's aiming area and before the shooter's arm gets tired and shaky from being held too long in the aiming position.

REFERENCE

1. Weston, P. B.: *The Handbook of Handgunning.* New York, Crown, 1968, p. 90.

Chapter 7

COMBAT TACTICS

AT the outset of any combat with armed opponents, police officers are at a disadvantage because their opponents have the advantage of the element of surprise. Under laws governing police behavior, the police officer must wait for an overt act indicating the opponent has a firearm or other deadly weapon and intends to use it against the officer. In addition, some situations demand that the police officer offers an armed opponent an opportunity to surrender, and only the opponent knows *before* he or she moves whether the act done will be surrender or an attempt to kill the officer.

The armed opponents of police officers usually make the decision of the place of combat, often selecting an advantageous location that puts the police officer at a disadvantage. Ambush attacks upon police officers are a classic illustration of an armed opponent preselecting the place of combat. Even when the police officer believes he has a positional advantage, armed opponents frequently withdraw along a planned escape route until they have drawn the police officer out of position in pursuit.

Police officers are sometimes outgunned by their opponents. Since 1960, the number of police attackers equipped with automatic weapons have been increasing. In theory, firepower or firearms superiority should be on the side of police. In reality, many police officers equipped with a service revolver have been confronted by opponents armed with rapid-firing shoulder weapons with large magazine capacities, many of them in the machine pistol class, capable of full automatic fire.

THE ELEMENT OF SURPRISE

Situation assessment and immediate action upon the police officer's evaluation of the situation is the primary defense against being surprised by an armed opponent.

Training officers in police academies across the nation have warned police recruits for years to evaluate the unusual and the unexpected as a suspicious circumstance and to act accordingly. While these instructors may outline grounds for such suspicion, the expertise that comes with being a working policeman over a span of time really develops in individual officers the key to survival: prompt recognition of some circumstance that is not "right."

Many police agencies imply by their regulations that the police on-duty holster for officers working in uniform is a fast-draw rig. This is not true. Safety and security are the major elements of these holsters. In addition, no fast draw in the world equals a keen and alert mind. In the bargain, there is no "sporting" need to give the other man an opportunity to "draw" first in police combat. Study situations which lead to trouble, learn to get the feel of a carful of youths as you approach them, learn to distinguish between a normal and abnormal "air" about a store as you enter it, and learn to be particularly careful with the "Who, me?" individual when persons are stopped for field interrogations.

Police officers, in answering radio alarms, may find the innocent-appearing family fight turns into a psychotic with a gun — and anxious to use it on anyone breaking up his "innocent" pastime of beating his wife — or an angry wife may develop when an officer remonstrates with her husband. This is true of any radio run: The "prowler" calls may be "Peeping Toms," but quite a few of them turn out to be burglars; and many of them are armed; the "shots fired" call may be children with fireworks, but could be a man fleeing the scene of a homicide; while the "felony-in-progress" call in most instances means nothing more than getting a description of the robbers for a radio alarm, some day the officer may get to the scene in time to meet several armed robbers as they take off.

Years ago, in New York City, I was put in charge of a CRMP car — Cruiser Radio Motor Patrol. These were cars in which three or four detectives prowled around high-crime areas and answered radio calls. A rule that had been put in years before required all detectives in this car to pile out with their guns in their hands on "jobs." All the doors opened as the car slid up to the call, and most of the detectives had one foot dragging the ground as the car ground to a stop, and exited in a running start. I thought it looked silly until we met three armed thugs fleeing a holdup scene.

In many cases, the police officer has some advance knowledge of what to expect when responding to a radio dispatch. Many radio broadcasts specify "Man with a gun" or "Criminal or criminals concerned are armed and dangerous." This is certainly reasonable cause for caution and a good, hard look at the situation upon arrival.

In large police departments, police intelligence units may alert officers to developing situations of danger, either by location, by naming specific individuals, or by citing the use of superior weapons by individuals or groups. In smaller police departments, individual officers or groups of officers may be forced to develop activity files showing areas likely to be dangerous in regard to armed attacks upon officers or the names of criminals likely to be armed and dangerous.

PSYCHOPATHS

"Psychos," as they are termed in police service, range from the psychotic to the psychopath, a person easily identified by a police officer. He or she may talk or shout excitedly and incoherently, pace rapidly back and forth, or impulsively attack and even attempt to kill an officer, but — and this is important — the officer has some warning. That is all any good cop asks.

Individuals with paranoid disorders or antisocial reactions are more difficult for a police officer to identify. A great many of the fatal attacks upon police officers can be blamed on these individuals and the fact that the police officer receives no prior warning of their intentions.

The paranoid, except for his delusional system, has a relatively intact personality with no outward evidence of any mental illness. The psychopath lacks ethical and moral development and an inability to follow the rules of approved behavior. These individuals are apparently intelligent, spontaneous, and very likeable on first acquaintance. They have an ability to put up a good front to impress others. What appears to be a man or woman with a likeable personality, a disarming manner, and an ability to win the friendship of others may very often be an individual with a callous disregard for the rights of others, unsympathetic, ungrateful, and remorseless in his dealings with police officers. They are utterly conscienceless in their attitude to law and order, and their homicidal attacks frequently have bizarre overtones.

Dave Salter, one of New York's top detectives, warned me about psychos when he was "breaking me in" on Third Avenue. There was a full moon that night, and Dave remarked that we might "get" a psycho or two. Dave explained that the area had a high percentage of psychos whenever the moon was full. "Watch 'em," Dave growled. "They're bastards that would kill you if they get a chance. Don't give it to them."

Young cops in those days didn't ask too many questions of older men in the job, but I queried how you could tell a psycho from a normal individual. "It's hard to describe," Dave admitted. "You get a feel for a situation; it's not right. The guy's too quiet, too polite, too ready to do what you tell him. Or maybe he's talking too fast, spilling his guts out, and at the same time his eyes never stand still. I guess it's the eyes that tell you the most, the little things too — a guy keeps wetting his lips with his tongue, taking deep breaths, wiping his hands on his coat or with a handkerchief, or he's sweating and it's winter... I dunno, you got to learn it."

AMBUSH ATTACKS ON POLICE

Surprise is one key element of an ambush attack upon a police officer. The other two elements are suddenness and lack of provocation.

An ambush is a fast-breaking event. It is initiated and concluded in a few seconds or no more than one or two minutes.

Lack of provocation means that the officer ambushed is attacked as a symbol of government and police power rather than as an individual. The majority of ambush attacks are random occurrences — Target Blue events are aimed at the police uniform or a police vehicle. Only a minority are likely to be attacks upon police officers known to the assailant and in which the motive is revenge.

Ambush countermeasures are complicated by the nature of police work and the demand for police services. Police cannot isolate themselves, because the delivery of police services requires contacts with all segments of the population and the police presence in every area of the community.

The greatest potential for risk reduction in ambush situations is a keen awareness of the environment in which the officer is working. In fact, the best defense against ambush attacks is the alertness of the officer prior to the attack. A "watchful" officer has a good chance of detecting possible ambush attack situations and taking defensive action to avoid, deter, or neutralize the attack.

Alertness to the danger of ambush attacks certainly warrants officers quickly evaluating the physical characteristics of a location for places of concealment an attacker might utilize and their potential fire zones. Every sense of the officer should be used to avoid being lured into one of these potential firing zones. Second, if the officer becomes suspicious, he or she should request help before proceeding. This is a cardinal rule in reducing risks from the threat of ambush attacks.[1, 2]

Cover: Concealment and Protection

When an officer is fired upon or about to be fired upon, one of the best combat shooting tactics is to take cover. It is the rare location that does not offer some cover for an officer under attack. Automobiles, portions of buildings, trees, telephone poles, water hydrants, large mail boxes, fences, and even shrubbery can be utilized as cover. Many of these places of full or partial concealment are particularly suited to various combat shooting positions, providing barricade-type support for two-handed shooting. A few of them have bullet-resistant qualities and offer positions of reasonable safety.

A British firearms expert, Colin Greenwood, notes that police officers are likely to be confronting desperate persons whose resistance to wounds and shock can be almost unbelievable, and officers fired upon or who believe they are about to be fired upon, should take cover rather than returning the fire from the open. Greenwood adds that an officer moving rapidly to cover is a difficult target even at short ranges, and that only in the rarest of circumstances, e.g. when it is not possible to take cover, should the officer return fire from the open.[3]

Taking cover before returning an assailant's fire has an additional tactical advantage for the police officer under surprise attack. The officer has some time to assess the situation and determine the most appropriate response under all the circumstances involved; the attacker has time to consider his or her own situation and may decide to halt the attack and surrender.

The Atlantic City (New Jersey) Police Department has developed a *Combat Confidence Course* in which officers are required to shoot at silhouette combat targets at short ranges from cover positions behind mailboxes, fire hydrants, telephone poles, and police vehicles. In developing this realistic training program in combat shooting, local research indicated attacks on police occurred at relatively short range, and a survey of various areas in Atlantic City revealed police officers usually have some natural cover in most shooting situations.[4]

NIGHT COMBAT TACTICS

As police officers we should level with ourselves and admit that aimed fire in the dark of night is not possible without revealing one's position to hostile fire from one's opponent.

I suggest night practice, holding a flashlight out at arm's length to provide illumination in which to see the target and the sights of the revolver, but every officer should realize the suicidal implications of this technique in a gunfight.

Police combat shooting is largely defensive, but in a few circumstances in which it may be termed a technique of offense — fleeing felons, barricaded killers, jailbreak attempts by felons — I believe the police should choose fire that does not jeopardize the life of a single officer. If the combat situation occurs at night and it is defensive, then the officer is at such close quarters and in such danger as to require defensive directed fire — and this is ideally suited to night shooting. If, on the other hand, the situation poses no immediate hazard to the officer, why expose a position by turning on a flashlight and banging away?

If the situation demands it, the officer has no alternative, but a radio alarm or teletype has brought back many a fleeing felon without injury to a single officer.

Night combat tactics worth practicing are as follows:

1. Two officers team up, one to handle the flashlight and the other the gun. The officer with the flashlight is "bait," and must turn the light on only for an instant, then move quickly to another position, where the maneuver is repeated. This has to be a fast-moving technique, and the officer with the gun must shoot while the scene is illuminated. It may be a very effective technique for officers working together in two-man radio cars.

2. The officer places his flashlight on the ground, or some other support, braces for a fast jump or two to the right or left, and then snaps on the flashlight and jumps. I have tried moving into a two-hand kneeling position after moving a few yards away from the light and was agreeably surprised that I could stay in the rear of the light beams and have my sights and the target sharply defined in the illumination from the flashlight. This is a technique to practice and to seriously consider, as the light is a "bait" that cannot be injured. Some officers may be reluctant to surrender their flashlight in a night combat situation, and, of course, this is a factor that must be considered, although it seems a minor consideration when the alternative solution may contribute to the accuracy of the criminal's fire.

An ideal device for night combat, increasingly used, is illumination of the scene with lights of the police vehicle. In this case, police officers dismount from the car and move to protected positions, if possible, before opening fire. A police officer can simulate these tactics by setting up a silhouette for night-time fire, then driving up in the car to the desired range, dis-mounting, and moving away from the area of return fire (the car) before starting to shoot. The key to safety in this instance is not only to move away from the car, but to also get set up for rapid, aimed fire before disclosing one's position by firing.

In any night firing situation, the police officer should copy the tactics of the military and change position frequently. Re-member the flash that accompanies the discharge of a cartridge is a tell-tale indication of your position. The firing of one or two shots, then moving fast to another position, and repeating this procedure may save an officer's life.

As a young policeman-shooter I tried various techniques for night firing, but none of them worked out. Old John Dietz, my first coach and former Olympic shooter, spent quite a few dol-lars on various self-illuminating paints which he daubed on my sights. However, eight to ten hours in a police holster meant that the paint lost most of its illumination factor.

As a sergeant on New York's East Side, I spent many a night prowling around roof tops in the tenement district. We had to play hide-and-seek with prowlers and burglars and some "psy-chos." Each tenement roof spans a width of about 20 feet, and then it raises into a 2-foot brick and mortar wall. This wall usually has two big chimneys along it; one at the front and the other toward the rear of the house. The criminals had nu-merous places to hide, and police officers had to examine each one as they progressed across the rooftops. It was rough work. We had several instances in which cops had been shot at point-blank range as they moved in upon a criminal's hiding place, or officers were pushed off of the roof by a sudden rush of a criminal from behind a chimney or wall.

Our usual technique was to use one officer with a flashlight and one as an "outrider." The officer with the light found a safe position (cover) and shined the light on the chimneys and walls just beyond the search area to back-light the rear of chim-neys and walls directly in front of the searching officers. Then the outrider moved along the edge of the roof farthest from the light and observed. The "lightman" watched the outrider, and at whatever silent signal meant "there he is," the light went out, and all hands moved to close quarters in the dark.

CLOSE COMBAT PROBLEMS

Close combat problems arise when the police officer is about 10 feet or less from his or her opponent. Many police officers have been killed and injured when they were within an arm's length of their opponent.

.One of the most dangerous encounters between a police officer and a suspect who may be armed and dangerous is either the initial or the final approach: when the officer advances to within close proximity of a subject to question or examine him initially or to frisk and possibly arrest him as the encounter progresses.

There is a definite hazard to closeness. First, if the officer has not drawn his weapon, the attacker may pin the officer's arm and prevent the use of the officer's weapon. Second, if the officer is pointing his weapon at the suspect, he or she may be disarmed.

Officers must be prepared for any rapid escalation of force by a suspect. This means the officer must allow space to maneuver and seek cover and/or draw his or her weapon. Within the limitations set by a police agency's regulations on the use of firearms, officers should be prepared to draw their weapons. It is better to be too early than too late.

The New York City Police Department has developed a close combat (hip) position in which the shooting hand is retracted to prevent possible disarming by a suspect who might seize the extended hand and weapon of an officer as the distance between them is diminished to an arm's length. In their training program, New York City's firearms instructors emphasize that this new position is not intended to replace the crouch (hip shooting) or point-shoulder positions but is a position desirable during the final close-range approach to a suspect who is suspected of being armed and dangerous.

In the close combat (hip) position, the officer's gun is much closer to his body than in the standard crouch hip shooting position, because the extended arm at close range might invite a struggle for the officer's weapon and possible disarming.

Aware that many officers approaching an armed and dangerous suspect keep their nonshooting hand extended from the shoulder to ward off any sudden lunge by a suspect, range officers supervising practice involving this close combat position require the free hand of the shooter to be placed behind the officer's back to negate the possibility of a self-inflicted gunshot wound during range practice.

Standard search procedures in United States police departments require officers to conduct a frisk of a suspect for weapons whenever they fear the suspect may be armed. Even after a suspect has relinquished a visible weapon in apparent surrender, these search procedures are required for the officer's safety.

The basic element of officer survival in these search procedures is to place the suspect off-balance. Suspects are told to lean against a wall, car, or tree with their legs and arms widely spread. Any attack upon the searching officer must be prefaced by pushing away from the leaning position. Since all such searches are conducted from the rear of the suspect, this movement of the suspect allows the officer to step back out of the reach of the suspect. Some officers keep one of their feet inside the right foot of the suspect, and any suspicious movement can be countered by a foot snap that throws the suspect off-balance or to the ground.

When there is no car, tree, or structure against which to position a suspect, the officer instructs the suspect to take a kneeling or pushup position as protection against sudden attacks. The pushup position in which only the suspect's toes and hands touch the ground is probably the safest position, as the weight of the suspect's body is on his extended arms. If the searching officer positions himself to the rear and out of reach of the suspect, any attempt to attack the officer is accompanied by adequate notice for the officer's protection.

DISARMING TECHNIQUES

If the criminal is within reach, or even "lunging reach," the police officer may think about disarming him. An overt move at this moment may panic the criminal into shooting when he might have willingly given up under a little persuasion. "Talking them down" from the high emotional level common at this moment should be attempted at first, and it will also give the officer a few precious moments to evaluate the opponent and the other circumstances surrounding the situation.

Actually, physical contact of the criminal's gun with the officer's body is the most advantageous position for the officer. It is necessary when the criminal is behind the officer — otherwise the officer cannot know the location of the weapon — and a big help when the approach is from the front.

Two steps are necessary in successful disarming techniques. One is to swivel the body away from the muzzle, and the other is to reach down and seize control of the weapon. Actually, the two movements can be made faster than the criminal opponent can react, but they have to be fast.

Once the officer has his or her hand or hands on the gun and has deflected the muzzle away from his body, the policeman has the advantage because the criminal's finger is in the trigger guard — he is caught unaware. A simple, wrenching motion of the gun away from the officer and inward upon the criminal's gun-holding arm, usually breaks the trigger finger or causes sufficient pain to force him to release his grip upon the gun.

Some police units teach a disarming technique that slides into a classic wristlock. In the wristlock, the officer slides one or both of his hands beyond the gun so that his thumb or thumbs are on the back of the criminals' gun-holding hand, then a slight upward, inward, and downward motion puts an untenable pressure upon the muscles controlling the fingers, and the criminal is forced to release his hold on the gun. However, at some point in this motion, the muzzle may be accidentally pointed at the officer's chest and head — a very undesirable feature of this disarming technique.

Another wrestling hold that is sometimes taught as a disarming technique is the armlock. The officer slides into a position where the pressure is exerted outward and to the rear in such a fashion that the pain causes the criminal to release his hold upon the weapon. This hold has the same disadvantage in that the arc of the weapon's muzzle as the officer moves into the final position of the hold may sweep across the officer's body for an instant — and that is too long.

While I advise every officer to try out wrestling holds and attempt to develop some skill with them before rejecting them, I sincerely ask that individual officers weigh their relative effectiveness against the more simple disarming technique of first swiveling the body out of the way of the gun's muzzle and then reaching for the gun and wresting it out of the criminal's grasp and studiously refraining from giving him any opportunity of again pointing it at any portion of the officer's body.

There is a possibility that a shot will be fired as the officer and criminal struggle for possession of the gun, but when it happens, the officer must have control of the muzzle. In wrenching a weapon away from a criminal by turning it in upon his trigger finger, there is a good chance of the criminal receiving a self-inflicted gunshot wound, but that is one of the disadvantages of facing up to a trained police officer.

I personally advise the technique of seizing control of the gun and its muzzle, as I consider this of primary importance in disarming. I also feel certain that it is easier to take a gun away from an individual than it is to hold onto the weapon. I also believe that a firm hold on a revolver keeps its cylinder from turning and thus jams it or causes the recoiling parts of an automatic pistol to be retarded to such an extent that a malfunction occurs and the automatic fails to function.

I don't believe that any sane man will attempt to cause a malfunction of a .45 caliber automatic pistol pointed at him by pressing on the front of it with sufficient pressure to hold it out of battery and thus cause a failure to fire when the trigger is pulled. This is living dangerously; I much prefer getting that muzzle away from the officer's body as the initial step in all disarming techniques.

Try out every disarming technique before settling on one that you think best suited to your own individual physique.

Practice it on a friend. However, do not practice taking the gun away by any sudden twisting against the trigger finger of a friend as any sudden movement — particularly when resisted, and all friends will resist — may cause a severe cut on the trigger finger. Try it out, but try it out slow and easy.

It is not amiss to point out that as the officer swings into position, with one or both hands on an opponent's gun, one foot and one knee can be put to effective use. A knee to an opponent's groin in a sudden, hard, rising motion assists any disarming technique, and while not quite so effective, a blow struck with a stamping motion of the officer's foot downward on an opponent's instep may also assist in disarming a criminal. In fact, either offense is a good defense against similar blows from the criminal.

The greatest obstacle to disarming a man is not so much the gun as it is the free hand of the criminal. It's amazing how fast a criminal can be disarmed, but if his free hand can reach any portion of the officer's clothing or body, it provides him with an anchor upon which he can level defensive pressure against the officer. It is vital, as the officer swings into the wrenching movement that will take the gun out of the hand of the criminal that he moves away from his opponent's free hand in order to leave him "swinging," that is, without any point against which he can lever a resisting pressure.

Officers should never forget that any criminal who has served time in any state prison is aware of these police disarming measures. In every prison yard in the United States, inmates teach each other disarming tactics, particularly emphasizing what to expect from police and how to counter these police tactics.

Finally, a nightstick in the right hand of a policeman facing an opponent with a gun in his right hand and a short distance from an officer is a natural for teeing off in what would probably be an arm-breaking blow. The position of the nightstick and the opponent's gun are the deciding factors as to whether or not the classic "baton" of the policeman can disarm an opponent. However, it must be remembered that the attack is to be delivered at the gun. Even a hard blow to the head of an opponent with a nightstick may not stun him rapidly enough to prevent the discharging of the weapon. I've seen nightsticks broken over the head of an enraged man without any apparent effect.

In disarming, get the gun. Then go after your opponent on more level terms.

PROBLEMS OF ATTACKS WITH
KNIVES AND CLUBS

The same friend or fellow officer with whom disarming techniques have been practiced can also serve in learning about knives and clubs. It breaks the monotony of practicing with a firearm, and the little additional time spent on this practice may someday save an officer a few cuts or bumps — and possibly fatal wounds. Almost every area of the country has in its police history a story or two about policemen being beaten with their own nightsticks, and in many areas police officers have been knifed in close-quarters combat with a knife-wielding assailant.

Clubs are usually swung downward at the officer, and the block is a simple one. An arm- or wristlock usually disarms the club swinger. On the other hand, a good knife man never swings downward with his weapon. He prefers straight lunges that are difficult to parry. Many of them are skilled at feinting an opponent off balance and "pull" an officer into "sucker" positions, if the policeman is not careful.

Seek local information from what might be termed native sources. Whenever called to the scene of a dispute or homicide in which a person has been knifed, in addition to securing the information called for by police procedures, the officer should query the witnesses concerning the exact techniques used to inflict the wound. He or she should ask about the preliminary skirmishing that is usually associated with knife fights.

Do not depend on the time worn cliché, "A gun can outshoot a knife." The assailant of a police officer is usually in the midst of a severe emotional storm: fear, anger, and frustration prepare a man to fight or flee. The normal body functions take over and prepare a human being for great muscular activity; the heart beats faster, blood vessels serving the exterior muscles of the body tend to become larger, and adrenalin is dumped into the blood to really charge up an individual. This physiological process can turn a common drunk into a superman for a few moments. A gun can certainly "outshoot" a knife, but it may not stop the knife-wielder in time. . .

A police sergeant and several officers were called to an altercation on New York's Bowery — an area frequented by homeless men and consisting mainly of "flophouses," missions, and cheap taverns. The police sergeant was first on the scene and found himself confronted by a man with a knife. Nothing about the man spelled out any menace, except the naked blade of the knife. It was a long, clean blade, and the derelict held it low; apparently just another wino, but the sergeant was cautious. He drew his revolver and ordered the bum to drop the knife.

"Ain't gonna do it," was the mumbled answer, and the derelict moved toward the sergeant. In all, nine shots were fired — six by the sergeant and three by an assisting officer, and the assailant was found upon postmortem examination to have enough lead in him to stop any normal man. But he wasn't normal at the moment of the assault; he was charged up with emotion and cheap wine. He succeeded in reaching the sergeant and stabbed him twice in the chest, inflicting wounds which proved fatal in a few minutes: A live policeman one moment, with every resource of the community at his command; the next moment, dead on arrival of assisting officers.

BODY ARMOR

Early "bulletproof vests" were so heavy and bulky that no one wore them, except on raids or in special operations against armed persons barricaded in buildings. While these vests had the capability of protecting officers wearing them against most handgun cartridges in the years before the Magnum loads were developed, they were never a factor in protecting an officer from surprise attacks, such as an ambush. The primary reason

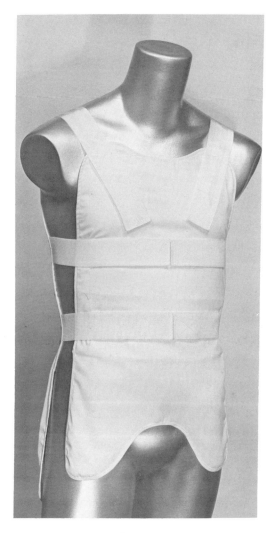

Figure 18. The Shirttail Armored Vest. The shirttail portion is not bullet resistant but helps stabilize the vest during exercise and enhances its appearance and comfort. Shoulder and chest straps are adjustable with Velcro® closures. The vest shown is manufactured by Safariland of Monrovia, California, and is also available in a women's model with the same shirttail features.

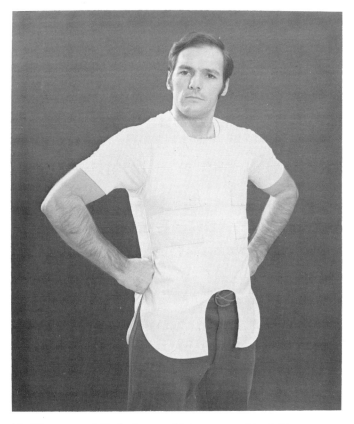

Figure 19. Wraparound Body Armor. This vest provides full torso protection: front, back, and rib-cage areas. The model shown is manufactured by Protective Materials Company, Seabrook, New Hampshire, and is part of their Flex-10® system offering two-for-one capability. On police duty where the hazards of armed attack are relatively low, the officer may elect to wear a single panel of Kevlar®. On higher-hazard duty, an extra panel of a special material providing protection against blunt trauma injury can be inserted in the carrier pocket of the vest.

is that they were usually in a police storeroom or in the trunk of a police car.

Modern body armor is comfortable, lightweight, and conceal-able. The majority of the models popular with police today may be classed as "soft" body armor: a bullet-resistant vest that clings closely to the contours of the body and can be worn under the shirt of a police officer (Figs. 18 and 19).

Blunt trauma is a bruise or other injury to the wearer of soft body armor. When a bullet strikes body armor, it exerts hundreds of foot-pounds of energy in a few thousandths of a second. While the body armor stops the bullet from penetrating into the body of the wearer, there is some effect on the body beneath the armor from the bullet's impact power. In most of the cases in which an officer's life has been saved by body armor, the bruising of the officer's body has been minimized and maximum publicity given to the fact that the officer was still alive.

The Law Enforcement Assistance Administration (LEAA) has supplied soft body armor to 3,000 police officers in fifteen cities across the nation as part of a $600,000 two-year field test. The soft body armor used in this field test is made by Kevlar®, a synthetic cloth said to be stronger than steel and lighter than nylon. It was developed as a substitute for steel in belted radial tires. Tests by the LEAA's National Institute of Law Enforcement and Criminal Justice indicate the armor is effective protection against 80 to 85 percent of all handguns.

Richard Davis, the inventor of Second Chance® body armor, responds to inquiries with a test sample and a letter instructing the inquiring officer how to conduct his own tests of its bullet-stopping qualities.

Safariland of Manrovia, California, claims their soft body armor resists more penetration than any comparable plain Kevlar pads. While Safariland's armor is based upon the energy absorbing qualities of Kevlar, this manufacturer claims that the addition of special meshes and other high-tensile strength materials supplement the basic Kevlar material. This manufacturer offers a considerable line of extended-coverage accessories, such as a groin protector.

Most manufacturers in the armor or body-protection field offer a featherweight model that stops most combat cartridges; a slightly heavier model that stops cartridges equal to .357 Magnums; and a heavyweight model that stops .44 Magnum bullets as well as 12-gauge slugs. Models are available for women as well as men.

Modern soft body armor now available to police is comfortable to wear, can be worn unobtrusively as an "undercover" garment, and has a proven record of bullet resistance. While a lightweight vest does not provide full protection, the important fact is that it is being worn by a police officer.

REFERENCES

1. The Police Weapons Center, International Association of Chief of Police: *Ambush Attacks: A Risk Reduction Manual for Police.* Gaithersburg, Maryland, International Association of Chiefs of Police, 1974, pp. 28-33.
2. Daley, R.: *Target Blue.* New York, Delacorte, 1973.
3. Greenwood, C.: *Tactics in the Police Use of Firearms.* Todmorden, Lancashire, England, H. Leah, 1969, pp. 9-10.
4. Clifton, R. R.: The Combat Confidence Course. *FBI Law Enforcement Bulletin, 46(4)*:3-7, 1977.

Chapter 8

COMBAT AUTOMATIC PISTOLS

COMBAT automatic pistols are recoil-operated, self-loading (autoloading) handguns designed for military or police use and chambered for the 9 mm* or .45 ACP† cartridges. Automatics designed primarily for the target range are generally eliminated from this classification because the close tolerance between moving parts of the weapon necessary to enhance their accuracy potential can lead to malfunctions under field conditions common to police service. Also eliminated are automatic pistols chambered for calibers under 9 mm, as these weapons of lesser caliber do not have sufficient stopping power to meet the demands of police officers and agencies in the United States.

In the past ten years, various combat automatic pistols have gained popularity with the police in the United States. Models 39 and 59 Smith and Wesson automatic pistols and the Browning Hi-Power® have become leading weapons in the 9 mm field. The Colt .45 caliber automatic pistol has always been a popular automatic pistol among military personnel but has only become popular among police in recent years. A runner-up in this combat automatic pistol field is the Colt Commander, now available in either 9 mm or .45 caliber.

At one time, police officers in the United States compared the combat efficiency of revolvers and automatic pistols generally; now it is necessary to compare combat revolvers with each of the combat automatic pistols. New characteristics of these automatic pistols include a double-action feature formerly associated only with the revolver and a massive firepower linked to a fourteen-cartridge magazine capacity. Formerly, police of-

---

*9 mm Luger or Parabellum. This is a military cartridge dating from 1901 and originally manufactured in Germany. It is now available commercially throughout the United States.

†.45 Automatic Colt Pistol. This cartridge dates back to 1911 when the United States Army adopted the .45 caliber Colt automatic pistol as its official side arm.

ficers switched from a revolver to a combat automatic pistol because of the shortcomings of the revolver; now they switch to "autos" because of their intrinsic merit.

SMITH AND WESSON 9 MM
AUTOLOADING PISTOLS

The full descriptive name of the Smith and Wesson Model 39 is 9 mm Autoloading Pistol (Double Action); the Model 59 is titled 9 mm 14-Shot Autoloading Pistol. The autoloading and double-action mechanism in both guns are the same, and the dimensions of the two weapons are practically the same:

Model	Barrel	Length Overall	Width Overall	Weight	Sight Radius
39	4″	7-7/16″	1-1/2″	26-1/2 oz.	5-1/2″
59	4″	7-7/16″	1-3/8″	27 oz.	5-1/2″

The shooting capabilities of both Models 39 and 59 are about the same. Both models have adjustable sights so that individual shooters can adjust the point of impact to correspond with the way they grip the gun and view the sights. The positioning of the trigger and its characteristics are the same in both models. Shooters who switch from one model to the other are pleased to find their index finger drops into the same position on the trigger of either the Model 39 or 59. I found the amount of slack and the trigger travel to be similar. However, some gun-smithing was necessary with my Model 59 to lighten the factory-adjusted trigger weight.

The major difference between Models 39 and 59 is in the grip or what might be termed the "feel" of the gun. Some shooters prefer the Model 39's backstrap with its curved and raised mainspring housing; others like the full-grip feeling inherent in the fourteen-cartridge magazine capacity of the Model 59 and its straight backstrap. Several sessions on the range would allow any shooter to adjust to either grip. A Pach-mayr® rubber grip for the Model 39 extends its grip dimensions for shooters who prefer a full grip similar to the Model 59

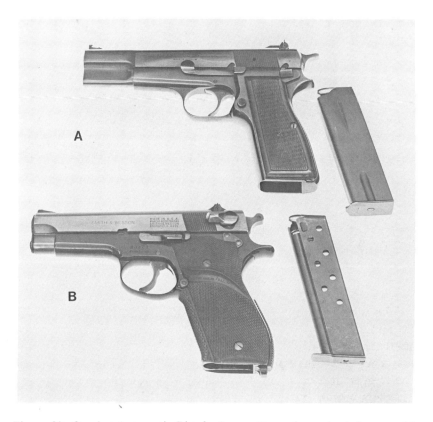

Figure 20. Combat Automatic Pistols: 9 mm. From the author's battery of 9 mm automatic pistols. (A) Browning 9 mm Hi-Power with its fourteen-cartridge magazine and factory-equipped walnut grips. (B) Smith and Wesson 9 mm Model 39 with its eight-cartridge magazine and Pachmayr "live" rubber grips. These grips are checkered and, unlike hard rubber grips, have a nonslip surface. Note the witness holes in the Smith and Wesson magazine: They are a visual indication of the number of cartridges in the magazine.

(Figs. 20 and 21).

As far as accuracy is concerned, I have shot several thousand cartridges from Models 39 and 59 and found both to have an equal potential for 5-X ring grouping of shots at 25 yards.

During my range firing of Models 39 and 59, I used factory ammunition commercially available from several manufacturers and only had malfunctions in the loading mechanism

Figure 21. The Smith and Wesson Model 59. This is a 9 mm fourteen-cartridge autoloading pistol. It is factory equipped with checkered high-impact molded nylon grips, an excellent 1/8-inch front sight, and a rear sight adjustable for windage.

when I accidentally purchased some hollow-pointed cartridges that were considerably shorter overall than the standard 9 mm Luger or Parabellum.

The safety devices built into the two 9 mm automatic pistols by Smith and Wesson have functioned well whenever I have tested them on the range. Magazine safeties on both models prevent firing when the magazine is out of the gun. I have heard rumors of some officers accidentally discharging a cartridge when they were loading or unloading one of these guns, but I have been unable to trace these stories to their source. Therefore, I can only report my own satisfactory experience with the safety features of these two weapons.

A choice between the two fine automatic pistols is based on an officer's desire for the firepower of the fourteen-cartridge magazine capacity of the Model 59.

THE BROWNING 9 MM HI-POWER

The Browning 9 mm Hi-Power has an autoloading mechanism similar to the foregoing Smith and Wesson automatic pistols. It has been officially adopted by the military services of several countries and a growing number of North American police agencies. To date, all models I have examined indicate high-quality workmanship, and tests have confirmed this visual inspection. This gun does not have a double-action feature, but it does have a fourteen-cartridge magazine capacity.

The Browning Hi-Power has dimensions similar to the Smith and Wesson Model 59, except that it is heavier and its overall length and sight radius is longer:

Barrel	Length Overall	Width Overall	Weight	Sight Radius
4-1/2″	7-3/4″	1-3/8″	32 oz.	6-3/8″ (adjustable sights) 6-5/16″ (fixed sights)

The Browning Hi-Power has a thick or "full" grip because of its fourteen-cartridge magazine capacity, but its lightly curved backstrap with a deep indentation just behind the trigger seems to fit this gun *into* the shooter's hand (*see* Fig. 20). In addition, this deep indentation shortens the reach necessary to position the trigger finger and makes it an ideal gun for officers with a small hand and/or short fingers but who want a 9 mm combat automatic with a fourteen-cartridge magazine capacity.

The accuracy of this gun through several months of range testing has been equal or slightly superior to the Smith and Wesson automatic pistols. It definitely has a 5-X ring capability at 25 yards. This pistol's accuracy may be due to its slightly greater weight or the longer sight radius or inherent in the rigidity of its barrel mounting.

I believe this gun is equal to the Smith and Wesson automatic pistols in freedom from malfunctions with factory-loaded commercial ammunition. In firing several thousand rounds in my Hi-Power, the only problems of malfunctioning have occurred when I failed to fully insert the magazine. Otherwise, its dependability has been unusual.

Some shooters thin out the upper portion of the factory-issue walnut grips to provide a slight rest for the thumb and a slight decrease in the reach for the trigger, but I did not find this necessary and like both the contours of these grips and their sharp checkering.

The Hi-Power has the standard safety features, including a magazine safety that prevents the gun from being fired when the magazine is removed. In addition, the manufacturer claims the loaded pistol will not discharge if dropped. I have tested the thumb and magazine safety on my own Browning 9 mm Hi-Power many times and found them to be safe, but since I do not like to drop any firearm, I have never tested this drop-safe feature.

I believe the fourteen-cartridge magazine capacity of the Hi-Power automatic pistol should be the first factor to be considered in weighing advantages and disadvantages. Then, the longer sight radius is a definite asset, and for shooters with small or short-fingered hands, the deep indentation in the backstrap and the short reach to the trigger are also advantages.

THE COLT .45 AUTOMATIC PISTOL

Among target shooters, the Gold Cup National Match® model is known for its accuracy, while the "service" model has always been known to need some adjustments to improve its accuracy potential. So-called accuracy jobs by the gunsmithing fraternity have been fairly standardized and can bring the military service model up to Gold Cup National Match levels. The manufacturer of this gun offers a happy medium, a weapon precision manufactured to shoot accurately. This is the Colt's

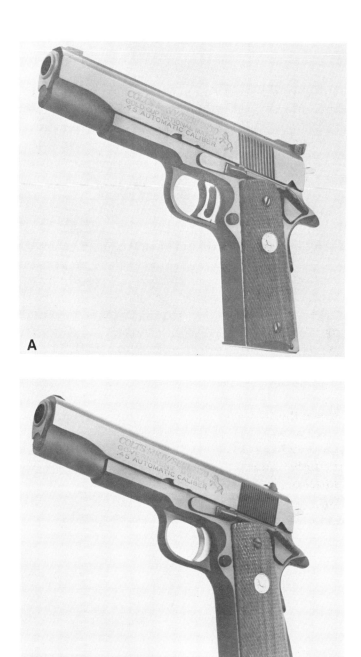

Figure 22. The Colt .45 Automatic Pistols. (A) The Gold Cup National Match model. (B) The Mk IV/Series '70 Government Model. These combat automatics are large in size, recoil, and stopping power.

Mk IV/Series '70 Government Model® (Fig. 22).

Many combat shooters believe that the tight fitting of the barrel and barrel bushing common to the Gold Cup National Match model or accurized service models may cause the weapon to malfunction under field conditions common to police duty. Even if this belief was only half-true, it would bar these guns from any consideration as combat weapons. The threat of malfunctions overrides the accuracy potential.

My gun experience has been that an accurized .45 Colt "service" automatic pistol functions well if it is kept cleaned and oiled. It is true that it may jam when it is first returned from the gunsmith, but some "shooting-in" on the practice range is a necessary postscript to this work. On the other hand, I have fired "service" pistols issued from a United States Navy or National Guard armory and have been unhappy with their lack of accuracy, particularly with the characteristic of these pistols "throwing" shots out of a group.

Any police officer selecting a Colt .45 automatic pistol for combat use (or being assigned one when it is the standard side arm of a police agency) should first make certain of the weapon's accuracy and then check it out for functioning with the ammunition likely to be carried on patrol. With this weapon, there must first be a certainty it will shoot where aimed and then a need for dependability.

I have had a few "smokestack" malfunctions with the .45 Colt automatic pistol: the just-ejected cartridge case caught upright in the ejection port. However, corrective action on the weapon or clip resolved the problem.

The basic dimensions of the Colt .45 automatic pistol are as follows:

Model	Barrel	Length Overall	Width Overall	Weight	Sight Radius
Gold Cup National Match	5"	8-3/4"	1-3/8"	38-1/2 oz.	6-3/4"
Government	5"	8-3/8"	1-3/8"	38 oz.	6-1/2

The grip of the Colt .45 combat automatic pistol is a large

one, but it is a grip that can be grasped comfortably by a majority of shooters. Unfortunately, it is not possible to shift this heavy-caliber weapon far from a grip with full coverage of the backstrap by the palm of the hand. The heavy recoil upon firing punishes the shooter if the weapon is centered on the last joint of the thumb rather than in the "V" between the thumb and index finger of the shooting hand. For this reason, persons with small hands or short fingers may have some difficulty in adjusting to this weapon.

The magazine capacity of the .45 ACP models is seven cartridges, but the magazine of the Government (Mk IV/Series '70) Model in 9 mm has been increased to nine cartridges.

The .45 automatic pistol has a very reliable thumb safety plus the grip safety, but the weapon can be fired when the magazine is removed. There is no magazine safety.

In northern California, there have been some instances reported of the .45 Colt automatic pistol firing accidentally when the weapon was in the holster, allegedly in a cocked-and-locked position, wounding the officers carrying them. Since tests by various military organizations over many years have revealed the thumb and grip safeties to be a reliable block to this kind of accidental firing, it is likely that the weapons involved in these accidents had a defective firing pin or firing-pin spring.

The .45 automatic pistol does not have a double-action capability. In the event of a misfire, the slide must be pulled to the rear to eject the cartridge that did not fire and to place a fresh cartridge in the chamber ready to fire. This requires a push-pull motion; a push forward with the shooting hand and a pull with the free hand against the resistance of a strong recoil spring.

When individuals or police agencies select the Colt .45 automatic pistol for police duty, the primary reason should be the man-stopping characteristics of the .45 cartridge. Despite its low velocity, the weight of the bullet and its diameter (cross-sectional density) offers the impact energy that led to the adoption of this weapon as the official side arm of the United States Army in 1911.

THE COLT COMMANDER

Years ago in New York City, police officers who wanted to carry a .45 Colt automatic pistol as an "undercover" gun would talk a gunsmith into chopping about 3/4 inch from the front end, and about 1/2 inch from the base or butt of a Colt .45 automatic pistol. It was termed a "short .45" and had a magazine capacity of five cartridges. It was an expensive modification, and dependability of the final product was dependent upon the gunsmith's skill in repositioning the barrel bushing, but for officers on hazardous duty in plainclothes who wanted the advantage of the .45 ACP's man-stopping capability (and perhaps the psychological advantage of the muzzle blast of these short .45s), it was well worth the money.

For some years, Colt Manufacturing Company's Firearms Division has been producing a shortened Colt .45 automatic pistol. This is the Commander model. It is now available in a Lightweight Commander® model as well as in a Combat Commander® of standard weight. An aluminum alloy frame reduces weight in the lightweight model, while an all-steel frame accounts for the weight in the heavier model. (The Combat Commander is now available in a 9 mm model with a nine-cartridge magazine capacity.)

The dimensions of the Commander models are as follows:

Model	Barrel	Length Overall	Width Overall	Weight	Sight Radius
Lightweight	4-1/4″	7-7/8″	1-1/4″	27 oz.	5-3/4″
Combat	4-1/4″	7-7/8″	1-1/4″	36 oz.	5-3/4″

The Commander models are equipped with the same two basic safeties as the larger Colt .45 automatic pistol: thumb and grip safeties. Commander models do not have magazine safeties. These guns will fire when the magazine is removed.

I have fired and carried as an off-duty weapon the Lightweight Commander from the time it was first placed on sale (Fig. 25). I know I have contributed to its popularity with many investigators in state and federal employ, particularly

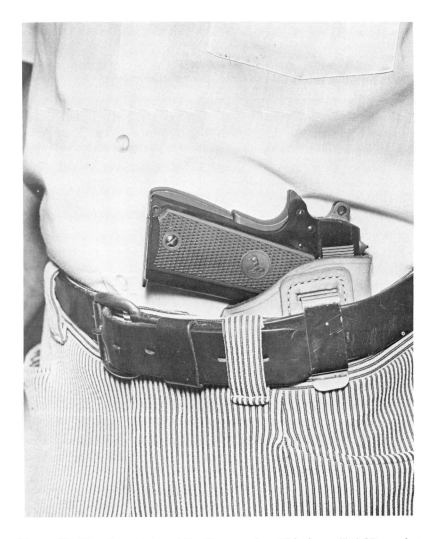

Figure 23. The Colt Lightweight Commander. This is a .45 ACP combat automatic of large caliber, small dimensions, and light weight. It is a shortened .45 Colt automatic pistol with a large grip. The gun shown is the author's Lightweight Commander in an inside-the-belt holster made by Bill Bacon (Bacon Holsters) of Rosemead, California. This is a fine gun for undercover officers. With a holster of this type and the large grip of the Commander, an officer has an excellent combination to speed up drawing and firing the weapon.

with those involved in the enforcement of laws relating to narcotic and dangerous drugs. It is lightweight and therefore comfortable to carry; its magazine capacity is sufficient for police conducting investigations, and, in my opinion, the .45 ACP cartridge is competitive with some of the weapons carried by contemporary drug-selling criminals.

In all of my range practice, I have never had a misfire or a malfunction with the Lightweight Commander, nor have I had any problems with its safety devices. (In the few instances I have carried it cocked and locked, my main worry was that I would remember to thumb the safety into off position if I had to use the gun.)

Accuracy of the Commander is not quite equal to the .45 automatic pistol; groups average about 1 inch larger at 25 yards range. The difference, however, in sight radius probably accounts for this, with the 27-ounce weight of my Commander Lightweight making some contribution. Do not forget that the Commander is the "little brother" of the Colt .45 automatic pistol. The larger gun's sight radius of 6 1/2 inches and weight of 38 ounces leads to smaller groups.

One of the frequently repeated criticisms of the Lightweight Commander is that this gun has a tremendous recoil and cannot be controlled from shot to shot. This is partially true and partially false. It does have a heavy recoil plus great muzzle blast. There is much more kick-and-whoom than the heavier Colt .45 automatic pistol with its 3/4-inch longer barrel. However, the Lightweight Commander in .45 ACP caliber can be controlled from shot to shot. This takes exercise and practice. Exercise with a rubber ball or exercising device to develop strength in the hands, and practice to groove a pattern of quick recovery from recoil, a rapid sighting and aiming, and no loss of time in starting the trigger pressure for the next shot.

I would not expect much more than the ability to get off five aimed shots in eight to ten seconds shooting the Lightweight Commander with a two-handed grip, but most reality-oriented combat shooters do not expect any greater rate of fire with any larger-caliber handgun of similar overall dimensions chambered for Magnum loads.

FINDINGS

Whether one of the foregoing combat automatic pistols is superior to the other reported upon depends on the circumstances under which a weapon will be carried: the combat conditions likely to be encountered in the police officer's working environment.

For instance, a narcotic squad undercover investigator does not require the accuracy inherent in a long sight radius, nor does he or she need the belly-poking overall length that accompanies any long sight radius. There is a need, however, in this field for a gun chambered for a man-stopping cartridge, because criminals on the drug scene are well armed and vicious. To my mind, the fast-breaking armed attacks on police working in this field call for a large-caliber weapon. Comfort is important but a lesser factor. Concealment was a factor at one time, but most police working in this field assume some underworld role as a "cover," and this warrants carrying a weapon without any great attempt at concealment. In fact, it might be out of character for an undercover agent in this field to appear to be, or claim to be, unarmed.

On the other hand, I fail to find justification for arming police patrol officers in a municipality without any unusual criminal population, resident or transient, with the heavy, bulky .45 Colt automatic pistol. Assuming the officers and their employer agreed on some type of automatic pistol as opposed to a revolver, I would suggest the Smith and Wesson or Browning 9 mm automatic pistols. These weapons have a reasonably long sight radius, are relatively light and without great bulk, and the 9 mm cartridge is earning an increasingly good reputation as a police combat cartridge.

The firepower of a 9 mm combat automatic pistol with a fourteen-cartridge magazine has considerable appeal to any police officer but is only justified when the officer's working environment contains the threat of ambush or other attacks in which the officer is likely to be surprised and the attackers armed with heavy-caliber, rapid-firing weapons. While the six additional 9 mm cartridges in the fourteen-cartridge magazine (as opposed to the eight-cartridge magazine of Smith and Wesson's Model 39) may not weigh a great deal at the beginning of a tour of police duty, they are likely to weigh a great deal more at the end of the tour — eight or ten hours later.

It should be noted that all of the combat automatics that have a magazine capacity of seven to nine cartridges also have a conveniently located magazine-release catch. The location and normal operation of these magazine releases permit a shooter to shift the shooting hand slightly when a magazine is empty and depress the catch with the thumb of his or her shooting hand and "pop out" the empty magazine. At the same time, the nonshooting hand can be ready with a loaded magazine. Sliding the new magazine into place and operating the slide to the rear to place a cartridge in the chamber ready to fire is only the work of seconds. (I know of one pistol instructor who teaches his students to count their shots so that a loaded cartridge is in the chamber as they replace magazines. This is a timesaver, as there is no need to pull the slide back, but I could never believe in its practical application under combat conditions.)

Conclusion

I have test fired the combat automatic pistols discussed in this chapter time and again. Handling and range firing over a lengthy period has led to a belief in their accuracy and reliability. There are now many other fine combat automatic pistols on the market. One model offers the double-action capability in a heavy automatic chambered for the .45 ACP. Any of these pistols may be as accurate and dependable as those reported upon in this chapter. There is certainly justification for any police officer to test such pistols against those discussed in order to have a basis for personal evaluation. When tests indicate a weapon has the necessary accuracy and dependability, the only factor to be considered is the availability of parts and repair services. When police agencies conduct the testing for a decision as to whether the weapon will be adopted as an official side arm of the agency, then consideration must be given to the availability of weapons for new recruits over a period of years.

Chapter 9

COMBAT REVOLVERS

POLICE revolvers, amazingly enough, are basically the same today as they were fifty years ago. Years ago, I sat down with Lt. John A. Dietz, former Olympic handgun champion, and he told me of his dreams for a new police handgun. Dietz frequently discussed his ideas with Harry Pope, the man who made super-accurate barrels, and they would call me in and we would discuss techniques for including the good features of self-loading "automatic" pistols in the design of a new revolver. Both Dietz and Pope agreed that the new weapon should provide a smoother trigger pull while maintaining the revolver's certainty of ignition and that the single-cartridge loading system must be changed or the capacity of a revolver's cylinder increased.

Today, both Dietz and Pope are dead, but the police revolvers have not been changed in any significant detail.

COLT REVOLVERS

Samuel Colt sent a description of his basic idea for a gun with a revolving and locking cylinder operated by cocking the gun's hammer to the United States Patent Office in 1832. From 1836 to 1841, Sam Colt produced revolving cylinder "pocket," "belt," and "holster" pistols at Paterson, New Jersey. However, the era of cartridge revolvers probably dates from the introduction of Colt's Peacemaker® or Frontier® model in 1872. This was the famed six-shooter in .45 caliber that became immensely popular along America's frontier. In 1877, the first double action made by Colt was marketed as the Colt New Double Action, Self-Cocking, Central-Fire, 6-Shot Revolver®.[1]

The standards Samuel Colt set for the precision engineering of the firearms bearing his name are still used and located in Hartford, Connecticut, and the Colt factory is producing "six-shooters'' designed to meet the needs of police officers seeking revolvers with both single- and double-action trigger mechanisms.

My favorite Colt revolver is a Python (Fig. 24). This is a .357 Magnum* firearm available in barrel lengths of 2 1/2, 4, and 6

Figure 24. The Colt .357 Python. This weapon is the top-of-the-line Colt revolver. Adjustable sights, a heavy and ribbed barrel with a shroud for the ejector rod, large and checkered walnut stocks, and precise fitting of moving parts are standard features of this revolver.

---

*Revolvers chambered for the .357 Magnum also fire the .38 Special cartridge.

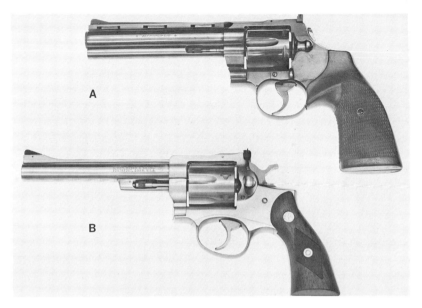

Figure 25. Two .357 Magnum Revolvers. (A) The author's Colt Python. This is the standard 6-inch barrel model, with Herrett's Shooting Star stocks, a despurred hammer, and Bill Davis's (Sacramento, California) gunsmithing job on the double-action trigger mechanism. (B) The author's Ruger Stainless .357 Security-Six as received from the factory. This is a good-looking, accurate, and dependable revolver that is competitive with the Colt Python in combat shooting.

Figure 25C. Ruger Stainless .357 Security-Six. Custom conversion by Bill Davis of Cake-Davis Company of Sacramento, California. This is an ultimate weapon for competition combat shooting among police officers and agencies. The Davis Bull Barrel brings the weight of this Ruger handgun to 52 ounces, and its accuracy potential is guaranteed: ten-shot group fired at 50 yards from a Ransom® machine rest with factory ammunition. *Note:* The accuracy of the factory barrel in this Ruger Stainless Security-Six can be equal to the Davis conversion and more than adequate to the demands of combat shooting, on or off the range. Competition combat shooters buy conversions for the psychological advantage — the knowledge that they have done all they can to insure mechanical perfection, and it is up to them to win matches.

inches. My Python has a 6-inch barrel with a sight radius of 7 5/8 inches and a total weight unloaded of 43 1/2 ounces. A pair of Herret's Shooting Star® walnut grips have been substituted for the factory grips. Recently, Bill Davis of Sacramento, California, gunsmith and part-owner of the Cake-Davis police equipment firm, took out the single-action capability and "tuned up" the double-action trigger mechanism. Bill Davis does not detail exactly what he does beyond chopping the hammer spur off, but it certainly shortens and speeds up the double action of this fine gun.

Other Colt revolvers are suitable as combat weapons for police officers; some of their features are the following:

Model	Caliber	Weight	Sight Radius	Barrel Length	Sights
Trooper Mk III®	.357	39 oz.	5-1/2″	4″	Adjustable
		42 oz.	7-1/2″	6″	
Lawman Mk III®	.357	32 oz.	3-3/4″	2″	Fixed
		35 oz.	5-1/4″	4″	Fixed
Diamondback®	.38 Spec.	24 oz.	3-7/8″	2-1/2″	Adjustable
		27-1/2 oz.	5-3/8″	4″	Adjustable
Police Positive®	.38 Spec.	26-1/2 oz.	5-1/2″	4″	Fixed

The Colt Police Positive is an old name in the Colt line but is now used for a brand-new Colt design. The top of the walnut grips are tapered and the bottom rounded. This, together with its small frame and weight (26 1/2 ounces as opposed to the Python's 4-inch barrel and 38 ounces) makes it an ideal .38 Special caliber weapon for officers with small hands or short fingers (Fig. 26).

Colt's trio of snub-nosed or off-duty revolvers all have six-cartridge capacity cylinders, 2-inch barrels, overall lengths of 6 5/8 to 6 7/8 inches, fixed sights, and are chambered for the .38 Special cartridge.

The Colt Agent® is the lightest model of the off-duty revolvers at 16 ounces. It has an aluminum alloy frame and small checkered walnut grips. The Colt Cobra® weighs 16 1/2 ounces. This revolver also has an aluminum frame but a large, well-proportioned set of grips. These are semicustom style,

Figure 26. Colt Police Positive Revolver. Copied from the Colt Detective Special snub-nosed revolver, this is a lightweight (26 1/2 ounces), medium-frame gun chambered for the .38 Special cartridge. Note the large stocks, unusual for a small-frame revolver.

filling the space behind the trigger guard well.

The Colt Detective Special® weighs 21 1/2 ounces. It has an all-steel frame, shrouded ejector rod, and a large, well-proportioned set of grips. These are not only semicustom style, filling the space behind the trigger guard, but they also lengthen the grip so that it offers a comfortable grip for a large hand. The Colt Detective Special has long been one of my favorite off-duty guns. It has an unusual natural pointing characteristic for a snub-nosed gun. The new semicustom grips

Figure 27. Colt Detective Special Revolver. A popular .38 Special snub-nosed gun with a 2-inch barrel, a six-cartridge capacity cylinder, and a grip that aids in drawing it from a holster and contributes to the weapon's accuracy.

have enhanced this feature (Fig. 27).

RUGER REVOLVERS

For the past twenty-six years, William B. "Bill" Ruger of Sturm, Ruger & Co., Inc., of Southport, Connecticut, has pioneered in gun design and manufacture. His product design and precision manufacturing has developed a line of police re-

volvers that is now competitive with the revolvers manufactured by America's two major handgun manufacturers: Colt
Firearms, and Smith and Wesson. Ruger revolvers are gaining
an increasing acceptance with police officers and agencies in
the United States.

The Ruger Security-Six® in .357 Magnum has become one of
the most popular large-caliber revolvers among police officers
and agencies in the United States. It is strong because of the
stainless steel used in its manufacture and its rugged design. It
has an unusual eye appeal because the polished finish on the
stainless steel is good-looking, and the semicheckered dark
walnut stocks contrast with this finish and add to its attractive
appearance (*see* Fig. 27).

The reputation of the Ruger Security-Six for 5-X ring accuracy at both 25 and 50 yards has been spreading. I think
Ruger's fine trigger mechanism has been one of the factors in
the accuracy potential of this gun. I've examined almost one
hundred of these guns and have found the single-action trigger
letoff clean and crisp and without apparent travel, and — more
important for combat shooters — the double-action trigger
pulls smooth, even, and with a crisp break off when the
hammer is released. I have found very little backslap or trigger
motion after the hammer is released.

With my Ruger Stainless Security-Six .357, I have been satisfied with the trigger mechanism in both single and double
action, firing it just as I received it from the factory. This is
unusual. I generally find fault and lighten the single-action
weight of the trigger pull and/or smooth out (and possibly shorten) the trigger motion of the double-action mechanism.

In addition, I like two other things about the Ruger double
action in the Stainless Security Six. One is that the cylinder is
both turned and locked in firing position before the final stage
of the double-action trigger motion is reached, and the other is
that the reach necessary to position the trigger finger is less
than in most revolvers.

The increasing use of the Ruger Stainless Security-Six

among police officers competing in combat-shooting matches indicates the potential of this revolver. Gunsmith J. M. Clark of Keithville, Louisiana, has put together a Clark Custom Ruger Combat Revolver® for competitive combat shooting matches. The major portion of this conversion is the installation of a heavy "Bull" barrel with a full-length Bo-Mar® rib and sight protectors (boosting the weight to a hefty 52 ounces). In one of his advertisements, Clark states, "The shorter reach from the grip to trigger makes the Ruger ideal for double-action combat competition."[2]

In my own range firing, I have found the accuracy of the Stainless Security-Six revolver equal to the Colt Python. This Ruger revolver has consistently grouped within the 5-X ring at 25 yards many times from all of the combat-shooting positions. While I have not had the opportunity to fire it extensively at 50 yards (and still argue that this range is beyond normal combat-shooting ranges in the reality of armed conflicts), it has grouped consistently well at this longer range, in and just out of the 5-X ring shooting in the two-handed "high" kneeling position.

The 7-7/8-inch sight radius of the 6-inch barrel model of the Stainless Security-Six is a fraction longer than that of the Colt Python. This, together with the 1/8-inch-wide front sight and the adjustable rear sight has contributed to my own accurate shooting with this revolver. In addition, I found the Ruger's weight and weight distribution to be remarkably similar to the Colt Python. In several sessions of range practice, I switched from one gun to the other several times and found the appearances of the sight picture and the general feel of the guns to be amazingly similar.

While the Stainless Security-Six in .357 Magnum is probably the favorite Ruger revolver among America's police officers, Ruger's snub-nosed (2-3/4-inch) barrel Speed-Six® has a tremendous potential as an undercover or off-duty weapon for police (Fig. 28).

The Ruger Speed-Six in .357 Magnum caliber is an all-steel gun of sufficient weight (31-1/2 ounces) and overall length (7-

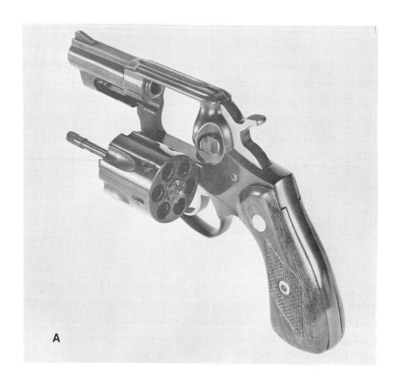

Figure 28. Ruger Speed-Six Revolver. A snub-nosed revolver that is chambered for the .357 Magnum cartridge. It has a 2 1/2-inch barrel and a six-cartridge capacity cylinder. (A) View with cylinder open, showing general rugged design and factory grips. (B) Side view showing Pachmayr Presentation grips of "live" rubber that enlarge the hand-contact area and make this short gun easier to control with Magnum loads.

1/2 inches) to handle the recoil of this Magnum cartridge. It is snub-nosed, but its barrel reaches out to 2-3/4 inches, a necessity to develop the .357's velocity potential and to handle the whiplike recoil of the .357 Magnum in short-barrel guns. The weight of the barrel and of the metal below the barrel that shrouds the ejector rod tends to make this fine revolver slightly muzzle-heavy, a favorable characteristic when shooting heavy loads in snub-nosed guns.

The sight radius of 4 3/8 inches makes the Ruger Speed-Six revolver slightly more accurate in aimed fire at 25 yards than the shorter and lighter Colt Detective Special. I found my Ruger Speed-Six grouped just in and out of the 5-X ring at 25 yards shooting double action from all of the combat-shooting positions. Since this revolver has the same basic mechanism as the Stainless Security-Six described previously, I found the single trigger letoff and double-action trigger pull to be very similar. Again, I made no attempt to change them.

Most of the shooting I have done with this gun has been double action from the point-shoulder position at 7 yards. Originally, I shot it with the round butt grips furnished with the gun, but soon changed to Pachmayr Presentation® grips of checkered nonslip rubber. The "live" quality of this rubber material, as well as the broad dimensions of this grip, cushions the shock of shooting .357 Magnums. As equipped, this gun can be fired rapidly with standard .357 Magnum cartridges. This rate of recovery from recoil is an important factor in combat shooting, particularly with snub-nosed .357 revolvers.

SMITH AND WESSON REVOLVERS

Smith and Wesson revolvers and pistols date from 1856 and the partnership of gunsmiths Horace Smith and Daniel B. Wesson. These two men joined forces in expectation of Samuel Colt's revolver monopoly expiring. Colt's basic patent expired in 1857, and since that date, both firms have been competitors in the handgun market. Daniel B. Wesson was apparently the prime mover in the continued success of Smith and Wesson in its early years. In 1874, he bought out his partner and became sole proprietor. The first double-action revolver produced by Smith and Wesson was a .38 marketed in 1880. This is the first in a long line of double-action revolvers of excellent design and workmanship.[3]

The K-frame of Smith and Wesson revolvers is designed to handle the .38 Special and the .357 Magnum cartridge; the N-frame is larger and heavier and excellent for shooting the .357, .41, and .44 Magnum cartridges. Police officers and agencies seeking a combat revolver with either a four- or six-inch barrel have an extensive array of Smith and Wesson revolvers on either the K- or the N-frame.

Most of the K-frame Smith and Wesson revolvers have checkered walnut service stocks. These grips follow the general outline of the metal frame to which they are attached (Fig. 29). The Smith and Wesson Model 19 .357 Magnum is a K-frame gun equipped with larger checkered walnut stocks that add to the size of the grip and fill up the gap behind the trigger guard (Fig. 30).

All of the K- and N-frame Smith and Wesson revolvers have a six-cartridge capacity cylinder and usually have a crisp single-action trigger letoff and smooth double-action trigger motion.

One of my favorite revolvers for combat shooting in .357 Magnum caliber is the Smith and Wesson Highway Patrolman.

Figure 29. Smith and Wesson Model 14 K-Masterpiece Revolver®. This is the K-frame model that is chambered for the .38 Special and was long popular with target shooters. Its accuracy and handling characteristics are making it popular with combat shooters.

Figure 30. Smith and Wesson Model 19 Combat Magnum. This is a popular on-duty revolver with United States' police officers and agencies. Its **K**-frame, 4-inch barrel, large stocks, and .357 Magnum caliber identify it as a combat revolver for police officers.

For several months it has been the revolver that I have used at twice-weekly range sessions. I've been shooting it just as it came from the factory with the exception of the grips. I changed to a pair of older Smith and Wesson grips of the same general dimensions as the factory issue but uncheckered. I could probably shoot just as well with the factory grips, but for my own comfort I prefer the smooth stocks (Fig. 31).

The accuracy potential of the Smith and Wesson Highway Patrolman is equal to similar guns of Colt and Ruger manufacture. Initially, I had to get used to its heavy weight (44 ounces) and the general bulk of the N-frame, but using the two-handed grip common to combat shooting fosters the ability to handle heavier guns. I have been shooting well in 5-X ring groups at 25 yards from all of the combat shooting positions and tight groups with only slightly greater dispersion at 50 yards from the prone position.

My favorite Smith and Wesson revolver is chambered for the

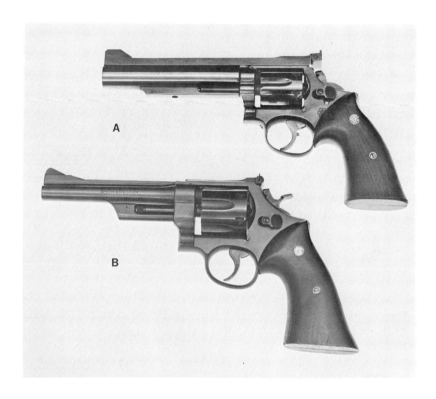

Figure 31. Two Smith and Wesson Combat Revolver. (A) Author's Military and Police Model revolver customized with a "Bull" barrel and Bo-Mar rib by Bill Davis of Sacramento, California. (B) The Highway Patrolman. A heavy frame (N) revolver designed for .357 Magnum cartridge and handles it with accuracy and a good recovery-from-recoil. Note that both guns have been stocked with an uncheckered version of Smith and Wesson large-sized walnut stocks.

.38 Special cartridge (*see* Fig. 31). It is an ancient, long-action Military and Police model that predates the present K-series of revolvers. I bought it from a policeman who had carried it as a 4-inch gun with fixed sights for many years — and that was many years ago. Now it has been converted by Bill Davis, of the Cake-Davis Company of Sacramento, California, to a combat shooting competition weapon. Bill added a "Bull" barrel and a Bo-Mar rib, and chopped off the hammer. Years ago, I converted this gun to double action only and installed a trigger stop in the rear of the trigger to curb backslap. I fire it with another old set of Smith and Wesson uncheckered grips. (The same style as I use on the Highway Patrolman.)

The "Bill Davis custom revolver" built around my Smith and Wesson Military and Police revolver has remarkable accuracy. After a few shots to sight it in, I began to get 5-X ring groups from all combat shooting positions at 25 yards, with several linked shots and an average size of less than 4 inches. In addition, the 50-ounce-plus weight is mainly forward of center, and this muzzle heaviness smothers the recoil of the .38 Special cartridge and allows rapid recovery between shots.

A gun modified for competition is not likely to get into the holster of an on-duty police officer; it cannot be considered an on-the-street combat revolver. It is a gun against which to test the accuracy and combat shooting characteristics of other revolvers.

Two Smith and Wesson snub-nosed revolvers with great popularity among undercover off-duty police officers are the Model 19 and Model 36. The Model 19 snub-nosed is a .357 Combat Magnum with a six-cartridge capacity cylinder and a round butt. This gun has an overall length of 7-1/2 inches and a weight of 31 ounces. The Model 36 is the Chiefs Special®. This gun has a small frame (J), is chambered for the .38 Special cartridge, and has a five-cartridge capacity, a 2- or 3-inch barrel, and a round butt. It has an overall length of 6 1/2 inches and a weight of 10 ounces with a 2-inch barrel. An airweight version of the .38 Chiefs Special is available at 14 ounces (Fig. 32).

The round butts of both of these guns are ideal for concealment while police officers are out of uniform: The roundness blends in with body contours under a shirt or coat. However, the lack of fullness in round-butt grips leaves something to be desired and does lead to some punishment when these guns are fired. This is true when shooting the .357 Magnum in the relatively heavy Model 19 or the .38 Special factory load in the light Chiefs Special. Unfortunately, I have not had the pleasure of shooting the 14-ounce Chiefs Special.

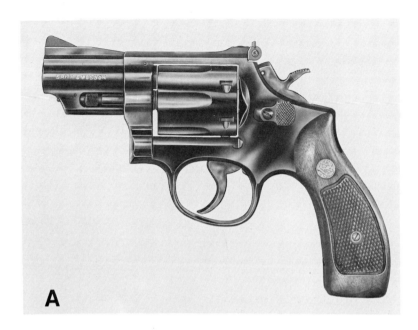

Figure 32. Two Smith and Wesson Snub-Nosed Revolvers. (A) The Model 19 in .357 Magnum caliber, 2 1/2-inch barrel, and round butt is a much-sought-after gun by undercover officers or for wear as an off-duty weapon. (B) The .38 Special, five-shot Chiefs Special is supersmall and light. It is the smallest effective snub-nosed revolver.

FINDINGS

Revolvers offer a very high potential for accuracy and dependability. They have long been favored by police as combat weapons. Since they have the capability of handling .357 Magnum loads, as well as the heavier .41 and .44 Magnum cartridges, the man-stopping capability of these guns is at the upper limits of any handgun.

Revolvers do not have the thumb safeties found on automatic pistols. Once a revolver is loaded, the basic mechanical safety is not to cock the gun and/or actuate the trigger until there is justification for doing so — in dry practice or on the range, in examining the weapon or in combat. Whether a revolver is safe when dropped, or whether the cylinder can be opened when the weapon is cocked — or the weapon not cocked when the cylinder is open — is somewhat in the nature of "fringe" safeties. The basic safety device on revolvers is the person handling one of them: not to cock the hammer of a loaded revolver or actuate the trigger in double action to cock the hammer until such action is warranted and safe.

Conclusion

I realize there are other major manufacturers of revolvers in the United States in addition to the three I have named in this chapter. In many instances, the revolvers of manufacturers other than Colt, Ruger, or Smith and Wesson may be equal or better in quality and performance, but this circumstance depends on individual testing. I confine my range shooting and testing to revolvers that have gained a reasonable acceptance with police officers and agencies in this country, and my comments on these guns are based on months — and sometimes years — of firing and testing. Since I do not believe that a short-range session with the gun or guns of a new manufacturer is as informative as I believe necessary, I suggest individual testing. This is also a good idea with any of the guns I have reported upon herein. Only individual test firing really informs a shooter of the characteristics of any gun.

REFERENCES

1. Chapel, C. E.: *Guns of the Old West.* New York, Coward, 1961, pp. 149-157, 232-239.
2. *The Police Marksman, 2,2*:46, 1977.
3. Parsons, J. E.: *Smith and Wesson Revolvers: The Pioneer Single Action Models.* New York, Morrow, 1957.

Chapter 10

SELECTION OF COMBAT WEAPONS

IN the delivery of police services, it is a common experience of most police officers to be exposed to situations of potential violence. Police training and tactics offer many procedures to resolve such situations without resorting to the use of the police side arm: the combat or service weapon.

In some instances, the police agency selects and supplies the service revolver or pistol; in others, the police agency establishes specifications of the manufacturer(s) and type of firearm that should be purchased by their officers. This is usually the case with off-duty or undercover weapons. Regardless of who makes the selection decision, or the limitations on this decision by regulations, the fact is that a revolver or pistol is a mechanical device. Since officers must place their faith and trust in this device under hazardous circumstances, it is reasonable to assume that any service revolver or pistol selected is the best and most effective of those currently available.

Unfortunately, selection decisions of the "best" combat revolver or pistol for police officers are often based on intuition, untested or unsupported hypotheses, unverifiable "expertise," and possibly some prejudice by someone according to his or her individual preferences. In addition, police management tends to include in the criteria upon which selection decisions are made the factor of "public reaction." Within the scope of their governmental responsibilities, this is no doubt a valid factor, but one difficult to understand by working police officers.

Another factor difficult for working police officers to understand is the prevailing-practices rationale. This involves a survey of the combat or service weapon of other police agencies to determine the caliber and type of firearm in use. If one caliber and/or type of weapon is in use by a majority of the outside police agencies surveyed, this is used as an argument to select the same weapon in the same caliber.

An examination of the staff studies of numerous police agencies concerning the relevant and valid factors that should be used in making a decision on the "best" revolver or pistol, among those currently available, reveals some commonality of criteria. The factors most commonly encountered in these studies are:

1. Reliability
2. Accuracy
3. Caliber
4. Firepower
5. Safety
6. Psychological advantage

RELIABILITY

The major argument among individuals favoring the revolver is its reliability. It will not "jam" as an automatic pistol may, and while some automatic pistols have a double-action feature, the total reliability of this feature is less than the revolver's reliability. The revolver shooter, in recovering from a misfire brings a fresh cartridge into firing position — rather than attempting to fire a cartridge that has already misfired.

ACCURACY

The mechanical ability of the type of revolvers and automatic pistols now currently available for police officers and agencies for review is beyond the holding abilities of most police officers: In machine rests, these guns are accurate. As a result, most of the accuracy potential turns to an analysis of the accuracy of a weapon in the hands of a police officer. The primary factor in this connection is the sight radius of a weapon and, since the sights are extensions of a weapon's barrel, the barrel length of a revolver or automatic pistol.

Heavy guns with 6-inch heavy barrels, such as the Colt Python, the Ruger Security-Six, and the Smith and Wesson N-frame revolvers, may have become popular because of their potential for accuracy. The fact that officers can rest the heavy gun upon the seat of a patrol car for a considerable portion of their on-duty time may also have been a factor in this popularity.

In combat shooting, the only advantage in a short barrel is the fact that the muzzle clears the lip of the holster a split second faster than a long barrel. On the other hand, the lengthy barrels have excellent pointing or punching characteristics for directed defense fire.

The sights of a handgun are an element in its accuracy. Colt, Ruger, and Smith and Wesson now offer as standard on most combat revolvers and pistols a good, broad (1/8-inch) front sight. The major difference in sight equipment is whether the sights are fixed or adjustable. Usually, on standard sighting equipment, the front sight is ramped to prevent its catching in the holster as the officer draws it, and the rear sight is well to the rear of the frame in a position permitting the holster to be cut away so that the projecting sight cannot "hang up."

Adjustable sights have the decided advantage over fixed sights in that they permit a shooter to adjust for his own eyes, grip, and general sight "picture" habits. Another factor, and of major importance, is the "square bar" effect which the flat top of the adjustable rear sight offers the eyes of a shooter (rather than a groove cut in the upper portion of the receiver). In aimed fire, it is much easier for a shooter to check against "canting," and numerous shooters also find they have less trouble in vertical alignment (top of front sight even with the top of the rear sight) with adjustable sights because of this horizontal line design of the top of these sights.

Fixed sights may not be off more than 1 or 2 inches between the point of impact and aiming area, but this distance may very well be the difference between life and death. Sometimes a police officer is in a position where one shot is meaningful. It may be the first round, it may be the last one, but if it lands accurately with damaging effect, it may prevent a criminal from firing a shot that would kill or injure the police officer.

CALIBER

The caliber of a firearm is the diameter of the inside (bore) of the barrel. It is usually expressed in hundredths of an inch or in millimeters (.38; 9 mm) and is measured from the higher interior surfaces (lands) of the barrel. There is a close relationship between caliber and so-called stopping power or the *incapacitation index*. High velocities are linked to the Magnum calibers (.357, .41, and .44) and heavy cross-sectional density is found only in the heavier-caliber bullets, such as the .45 ACP.

In the calibers in which revolvers are chambered, there is a definite trend to revolvers chambered for the .357 Magnum and some indications that the .41 Magnum — and even the .44 Magnum — are not unsuited to the needs of police officers.

However, on the police management level, many police chiefs feel that the .357 cartridge is too powerful for built-up communities: The bullet will go through wall after wall. It is true that the .357 Magnum has greater penetration than the .38 Special, and it will go through several walls of a tenement or a small home, but whether or not this is a logical argument against the use of this fine cartridge is open to debate. It is certainly a fine argument for using it in attacks upon fleeing automobiles or in overcoming the resistance of armed, barricaded persons.

In the normal .38 Special, the police bullet is all lead, round-nosed, and weighs 158 grains. It has excellent penetrations and fair stopping qualities. This cartridge is also available with a 200-grain round-nosed bullet for police use, and though it lacks penetrating qualities, it delivers greater impact energy due to the increased bullet weight.

The bore diameter of a revolver chambered for the .38 Special is within a few thousandths of an inch of .357 — despite the fact they have always been known as .38s and thus implied a bore diameter of .380. The .357 Magnum cartridge is actually a high-velocity ".38" load, as it is sized for the same bore diameter. However, to guard against accidents, the new cartridge case was designed 0.135 inches longer than the standard .38 Special case. The diameter of the new cartridge case remained the same as the .38 Special. These two design features meant that the .357 Magnum could not be fired accidentally in a weapon chambered for the .38 Special, as the extra cartridge length precludes closing the cylinder, but any .38 Special cartridge can be fired safely in the .357 Magnum revolver.

The excessive recoil of the .357 Magnum does slow down rapidity of fire and must be considered in selection of a revolver. The "whoom" and the wallop of the recoil jars anyone shooting this heavy caliber for the first time, and while practice overcomes the shock of the loud report, no amount of shooting seems to overcome the effect of recoil.

Of course, the additional impact power of the .357 Magnum compensates for excessive recoil, but it is something to be considered in police combat shooting, as it slows down recovery of aim and, therefore, delivery of accurate fire.

Excessive recoil is not too meaningful in double-action shooting from the hip or from any of the two-hand, kneeling positions. In double-action aimed fire, this recoil bounce is less noticeable than in single-action fire, due to the fact that the thumb is carried in a low position and locked in place.

There is no question that most officers can fire more shots in the same amount of time with a .38 Special than they can with a .357 Magnum — and there is always a feeling that there is more personal safety in six shots than there is in four shots. Roughly, this is the ratio: six to four. Experience and practice — and two-hand positions — can move this up to six to five. In other words an officer can learn to shoot five .357 Magnum rounds in the same time he can get off six .38 Special cartridges. This is also true, and to a greater extent, when shooting the .41 and .44 Magnum revolvers or the .45 caliber automatic pistol.

Impact energy, or the force producing the "knock-down" or "man-stopper" capability is important to police. The three major factors in determining the impact energy of any bullet are the bullet's weight, its shape, and the speed at which it is moving. If a 158-grain bullet and a 200-grain bullet of the same basic shape are moving at identical velocities, then the heavier bullet has more impact energy. However, if the velocity of the lighter bullet is stepped up a few thousand feet per second

(FPS), then the lighter bullet can equal the impact energy of the heavier projectile at slower speeds.

The "knock-'em-down" characteristics of the .357 Magnum, as compared to the .38 Special, can be readily visualized by the fact that the .357 Magnum 158-grain lead bullet achieves a velocity of 1450 FPS, as opposed to the 870 FPS normal velocity of the same bullet in .38 Special caliber. This increase in velocity gives the .357 Magnum a muzzle energy of 690 foot-pounds, compared to the 266 foot-pounds of muzzle energy of the .38 Special: almost three times as much impact power.

In diameter, the 9 mm bullet is linked to the .38 or .357, but it has a velocity at the muzzle (1120 FPS with metal-case bullets) that is above the average .38 Special and below the 1400 to 1700 FPS potential of the .357 Magnum.

On the other hand, the .45 ACP is a slow-moving load. The .45 ACP metal-case bullet of 230 grains moves at a sedate 850 FPS, but its weight and cross-sectional density make up for this low velocity.

Bullets in the various calibers range from full-metal cases (jackets) to hollow points, with intervening styles of all-lead and soft-point bullets.

At one time, humanitarian concepts in the police service prevailed against any use of the hollow-point bullet because it was classed as the traditional "dum-dum" bullet, forbidden to military forces in many countries. However, the fact that police officers found many criminals were using hollow-point bullets in attacks on police officers lead to some reappraisal. The turning point in the decision to use hollow-point bullets by many police officers or to allow their use by police management was the discovery that the hollow-point bullet has a low potential for ricochets. As one extensive Law Enforcement Assistance Administration study reported, "Hollow-point bullets are less likely than lead bullets to penetrate the body entirely and then ricochet to strike bystanders."

Strangely, the alleged potential of hollow-point bullets to expand upon impact and to cause massive wounding has led some police officers to forego their use; the discovery that these bullets at handgun velocities do not expand as claimed has led others to use other bullets.

This later circumstance may be due to the fact that handgun velocities claimed by ammunition manufacturers require barrels at least 6 inches in length and do not consider the energy loss among the gases of the cartridge ignition that escape from the gap between the front of the cylinder and the rear of the barrel in revolvers.

The caliber most appropriate to police weapons is one that provides adequate protection to the citizens of a community and the police officers serving it. While the most important characteristic in relation to the caliber of a weapon for police combat is so-called shocking power or incapacitation index, it should be remembered that sufficient power to *stop immediately* the most determined criminals and keep them from completing any criminal attack may be an end-of-the-rainbow goal. Hate, anger, and other emotional forces may power some individuals despite massive gunshot wounds. In addition, stopping the action of an opponent immediately may require wounds in certain portions of the human body, and any slight deviations negate the alleged stopping power of the gun and cartridge concerned.

FIREPOWER

The firepower of a handgun is linked with the number of cartridges that can be fired without reloading the weapon. To some extent, there is a joinder between this characteristic and the speed that the weapon can be reloaded under combat conditions.

It can be readily seen that the combat automatic pistols with fourteen-cartridge magazine capacity have superior firepower. This is supplemented by the fact that magazine (clip) reloading in these guns is a speedy process under any conditions.

Speed reloaders for revolvers have upped the firepower potential of these weapons, but the capacity of most revolver cylinders is still no more than six cartridges.

SAFETY

Revolvers and automatic pistols are equally safe. However, police officers must be trained in the more complex safety problems of automatic pistols.

There is some merit to the claim that automatic pistols have one basic and unsafe characteristic, and this is that they must be carried in a police officer's holster cocked and locked as the conditions of armed combat require a weapon to have a basic availability for immediate use. However, manufacturers claim their automatic pistols can be safely carried in this manner, and many military and police personnel have carried them in this fashion without accident.

PSYCHOLOGICAL ADVANTAGE

Officers are at a psychological *disadvantage* in any confrontation with an armed opponent if they believe their service weapon has poor shocking power, slow reloading time, and less firepower than the opponent's weapon or called for by the combat situation. For instance, an officer armed with a .38 Special revolver would be at a psychological *disadvantage* if he or she was ambushed by two opponents armed with 9 mm or .45 ACP automatic pistols with fourteen-cartridge magazines or some military weapon of equal or greater firepower.

Ideally, the psychological *advantage* favors a police officer armed with a weapon that stops the attack of an armed opponent with no more than two bullets in the opponent's torso area, meaning: "Stop the attacker from whatever he or she is doing *immediately.*"

Under some circumstances in urban area policing, the psychological *advantage* favors a police officer armed with a revolver or pistol of sufficient caliber to disable an opponent with a minimum amount of shots but, at the same time, protects the public from stray bullets that ricochet from hard surfaces or penetrate through and range far beyond the opponent.

Reliability may be a major factor in achieving a psychological *advantage.* The knowledge that a revolver or automatic pistol can be depended upon may be the basis upon which officers can build a belief in their combat weapon, and anything that reassures an officer that his or her weapon is adequate to the demands of the immediate or expected combat situation enhances this factor.

POLICE SERVICE WEAPONS AS SAFETY EQUIPMENT

The Oakland (California) Police Officers Association and certain police officers sought a writ of mandamus and declaratory relief in California's Superior Court directing that the city of Oakland furnish its police officers without charge various safety equipment, including service revolvers. The trial judge in Superior Court ruled against them, but the California Court of Appeals reversed the trial court, holding that a police service revolver is a "safety device" within the meaning of California's Labor Code and that such devices should be furnished by employers as required by the Labor Code.

The California Court of Appeals opinion states:

> It is difficult to conceive of equipment which is more protective in nature than the officer's revolver. To be sure, its best use is during its presence in his holster. But while it is so contained, it enables the officer to make arrests, to interrogate suspects, and to carry on his multifarious duties with the knowledge that if there develop serious resistance or threat of danger, he can protect himself even against more than one potential assailant. Occasionally, he may actually use the weapon when he is not in personal danger, as in shooting at a fleeing felon, although even in such cases often he must beware lest the felon be armed and turn upon him, or that confederates of the fugitive be ready for attack. But the use of the weapon against fugitives is but a small part of the usefulness of the revolver. The gun provides effective means of law enforcement because it continually gives a measure of safety to the officer.[1]

REFERENCE

1. Oakland Police Officers Association *et al.* v. City of Oakland, 30 C.A. 3rd, 106 Cal. Rptr. 134 (1973).

Chapter 11

HOLSTERS

THERE is no "best" holster for every occasion. There has to be a compromise between concealment, safety, and speed. An ankle holster is particularly suited to officers working on vice and gambling cases. They must be armed, but they do not want a "bump frisk" to reveal the fact they are carrying a gun. A district attorney's man may be involved in hand-to-hand encounters, but the use of a weapon is not justified until his life is actually endangered — this man requires a safety snap-fastener to keep his gun in the holster until he needs it. On the other hand, a federal agent working on the apprehension of armed fugitives wanted in connection with serious felonies such as homicide and kidnapping needs a holster designed for top speed.

The needs of police officers performing uniformed patrol must also be considered; these men must have safety built into the design and construction of their holsters. They want a holster from which it is difficult for a criminal or psychopath to "snatch" their service revolver, but from which they may draw it with dispatch.

There is, however, no excuse for insisting that police officers wear their revolvers in holsters worn underneath a long, suit-type coat. This is tantamount to leaving the gun back in their lockers at the police station.

I know that many police departments have experimented with outside holsters and junked them because an officer's gun was snatched during some patrol encounter, and while I doubt if an objective investigation would reveal the outside holster as the major factor in a tragedy such as this, I also know that among my own friends there are quite a few who do not believe in outside holsters for police officers.

If the head of a police unit insists on officers carrying their service revolvers under a full-length coat, he or she should have a uniform designer provide suitable vents in the coat giving access to the officer's revolver and supplement this designing technique by orders as to just what portion of the officer's body should be used in positioning his holster. It is silly to have vents cut in the right rear of a uniform jacket and then have officers positioning their holsters at the left- or right-front body area.

DIRECTIONAL DRAW

There is a directional-draw factor in all holsters. The best directional draw results when the muzzle of the revolver is pointed at the target just as it clears the holster. The holster has presented the weapon to the shooter in such a manner that he draws almost in line with the direction in which he intends to shoot.

The officer who is facing his target and draws from a hip holster has a very good directional draw — as the gun clears the holster, it is moving through a short arc that brings it to bear on the target. On the other hand, a shooter equipped with a shoulder holster and with his target far to his own right has to bring his muzzle through an arc of almost 180° before he is pointed in the direction he intends to shoot. However, if the target was to his own left front, then a shoulder holster would offer good directional draw characteristics. This is also true of cross-draw holsters and other special rigs. If the target is to one side, then there is a definite advantage, but if the target is away from the direction of the muzzle as it clears the holster, then the shooter is at a disadvantage. The holster that offers the best directional draw on all targets is the hip holster (Fig. 33).

HOLSTERS FOR UNIFORMED DUTY

Good-looking leather equipment can dress up the uniform of any police officer. I think the most tragic neglect in police management in this country has been the failure to develop the psychological threat inherent in a workmanlike display of police

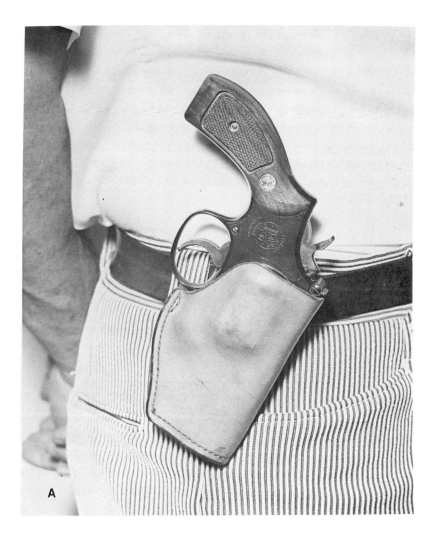

Figure 33. Hip Holsters. These holsters have excellent directional-draw characteristics. (A) A sturdy open-top holster made by Herrett's of Twin Falls, Idaho. (B) A low-silhouette design by Safariland, Monrovia, California, that eliminates the bulge where the belt joins the holster and holds the gun close to the body. This holster has a thumb-break safety, which is safe but easily operated when drawing the gun.

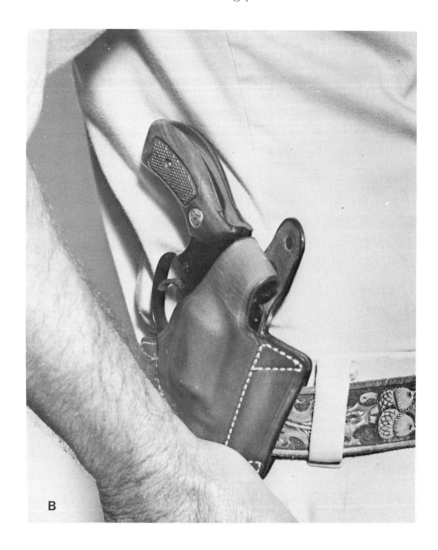

Figure 33B.

C

Figure 33C. Shoulder Holster. The Jackass® shoulder holster system: holster, harness, and cartridge pouches. Designed for snub-nosed revolvers, this shoulder rig offers the butt of revolvers such as the Smith and Wesson Chiefs Special shown for a rapid draw. There is little give in this harness, as the straps across the shoulders can be adjusted, as can the strap at the rear joining the two shoulder straps. Cartridge pouches shown are for loose cartridges, but these holders could be adapted to speed-loading devices or strip loaders, or clips for automatic pistols. It is manufactured by the Jackass Leather Company, Glenview, Illinois.

equipment designed to suppress crime and criminals (Fig. 34).

I think a revolver and handcuffs where the public can see them tells this story: I'm not out here just to direct traffic, or ride around looking for cases of public intoxication, or even to adjudicate minor altercations; *I'm out here to arrest and apprehend the roughest, toughest criminals who attempt to prey upon anyone in this community!*

The argument in favor of covering up a gun with a coat, jacket, or holster flap based on the plea that it is necessary protection from rain and snow is a specious one. It is the officer that needs protection. A gun can always be cleaned, and swabbing out gunshot wounds is not necessary when a gun is readily available.

The odd miscellany of gun rigs presented to the public on hot summer days when officers strip off their coats in localities in which the holsters are hidden by coats or jackets, is the best argument in favor of outside holsters.

Modern holsters for police officers on uniform duty angle the butt to the front for ease of drawing the weapon, are contoured to fit close to the body in the hip area, and position the butt of the weapon away from the body for quick access. This latter feature is a valuable assist to the uniformed officer.

GIMMICK HOLSTERS

Springs and other metallic devices for retaining a revolver in its holster are invitations to self-destruction. Holsters requiring the trigger finger to be placed in the trigger guard to operate a release are particularly dangerous. An officer should not put a finger in the trigger guard until the muzzle of the revolver or pistol has cleared his or her body and started to move toward the opponent or a target.

"Clamshell" holsters, and others that require an officer to punch a finger through a small opening, or against a small-sized hidden button, may be deadly in the excitement of drawing a gun when a criminal is shooting at the officer or about to shoot at him or her. Some officers whom I've interrogated on this score admitted that in several instances they became excited

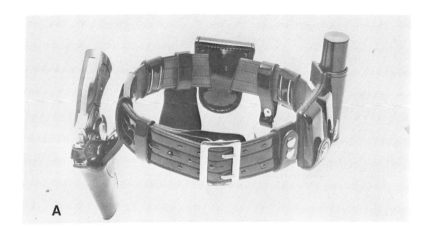

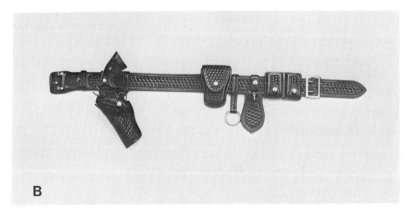

Figure 34. Holsters for Uniform Duty. (A and B) Two attractive and functional police assemblies: belt, holster, and holders for accessories. (C) A swivel holster of good appearance and an easily unfastened safety strap. (D) A holster with a thumb-break safety strap. Note that this holster is designed for positioning the gun away from the body. All leather products pictured are by Bianchi Leather Products, Temecula, California.

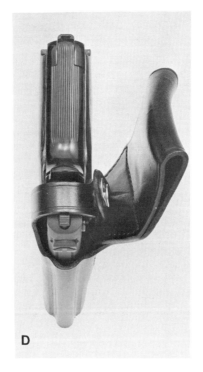

Figure 34C and D.

and "forgot" about the release. However, these invariably involved officers who had carried their weapon in plain holsters for many years before buying the gimmick holster. A new officer with no prior experience with other holsters would not have this difficulty but would still have to play blindman's bluff with the hole or the button in order to get the weapon into action. It is not just a case of drawing the gun; it's a case of poking or pressing the release and then drawing the weapon.

Some of the self-opening holsters rely on pressure in a certain direction on the butt of the revolver in order to release a retaining device. A "psycho" attempting to wrench the gun from the officer's holster might hit on the right "combination" and get the gun without any effort. There have also been cases of motorcycle officers having to turn around and pick up their revolver on the third or fourth bounce — either the wind or some pressure of their elbow activated the holster release.

Another officer described an interesting experience with one of the gimmick holsters. He had drawn his gun in expectation of an attack by an armed teen-ager, but when the youth fled, the policeman hesitated to shoot because of his age. In the course of a three-block chase, the officer tried several times to put the weapon back in the holster, but could not do so at a run — and since he wanted to catch the youth he kept running — with the holster flapping like a loose sail.

HIDEOUT HOLSTERS

A hideout holster can be positioned anywhere on the body. Years ago a typical hideout was an ordinary holster sewn to a square piece of leather and shoved into a detective's rear hip pocket. This holster was retained in position by a small piece of leather which buttoned over the hip-pocket button thoughtfully provided in those days by most tailors — but not to anchor holsters. Another was termed a shoulder holster and this hung the weapon in the armpit with a complex system of leather and elastic that felt like a friendly wrestler had applied a full nelson.

In modern holster design, hideout holsters are generally

grouped into the following types: hip, shoulder, belly, cross-draw, and holdout.

HIP HOLSTERS: These holsters provide a very fast and accessible draw. FBI agents and other federal law enforcement officers favor the hip holster (Fig. 35).

The hip holster is also the most suitable holster for running the Practical Pistol Course — the only one permitted by many range officers conducting combat courses of draw-and-fire practice. Other holsters position the gun so that shooters on adjoining firing points may be endangered as the weapon is drawn. In drawing from a hip holster, the shooter moves the gun through an arc starting at his side and ending down-range, and therefore does not endanger other shooters.

The holster is usually positioned just to the rear of the center line of the officer's body and offers the gun to the officer butt first. That is, the butt is forward as the gun is worn, and the muzzle is to the rear. A 10° angle is sufficient to assist in a fast draw, but many officers and agents prefer holsters that slant the gun forward as much as 60°.

SHOULDER HOLSTERS: Usually these holsters are positioned so that the barrel is almost vertical, the muzzle of the gun is just above the belt line, and the butt is within the armpit area. The weapon is held in place with a leather-covered piece of spring steel gripping the revolver around the cylinder. In drawing, the weapon is pulled out against the pressure of the spring. This is not a gimmick holster. A semicircular-shaped flat spring with an open end toward the direction of the draw is the retaining device.

These holsters provide good concealment, some speed, and effective retention of the weapon. However, before the motion of drawing the weapon even starts to move the gun, the slack of the harness has to be worked out and the tension of the spring must be overcome. Then, when the gun moves, the officer must put the brakes on as he attempts to point the muzzle in the direction in which he wants to shoot.

A new and innovative shoulder harness includes a handcuff case, locating it so that it balances the weight of the gun in the holster. This should make this rig more comfortable and at the

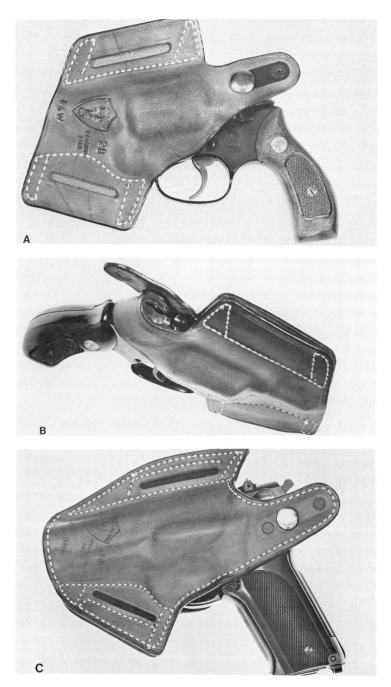

Figure 35. Hip Holster. Three views of a high-rise and low-silhouette holster by Safariland of Monrovia, California. (A) Belt loops are at bottom of holster and well spaced. They place the gun high against the wearer's rib cage and pull it in against the body. (B) Thumb-break safety strap holds gun in position, but can be quickly released in the motion of drawing the weapon. (C) This holster minimizes the bulk of 9 mm automatic pistols. This design also affords maximum concealment to the large (.45 ACP) automatic pistols.

same time reduce the slack in the shoulder harness when the gun is drawn.

BELLY HOLSTERS: These rigs were so named because they fit inside the belt of an officer. They are equipped with a metal clip or a loop of leather joined with a snap fastener for attaching to the belt of a wearer. Such holsters are not equipped with any retaining device, as they depend on the compression of the gun between the waist belt of the wearer and the soft flesh of the abdominal area to retain the gun in the holster ready for instant use (*see* Fig. 36A).

Belly holsters can be worn in the right front of the body with the butt to the rear for right-handed shooters or in a cross-draw position. In any event, any barrel longer than 2 inches usually causes a rude, probing sensation in the groin area when the officer sits down; even a 2-inch barrel sometimes needs a little adjusting when the officer gets into a car.

Belly holsters are ideal in hot weather when a jacket is not normally worn; a light sports shirt can be worn outside the pants. The shirt drapes over the gun and holster and provides

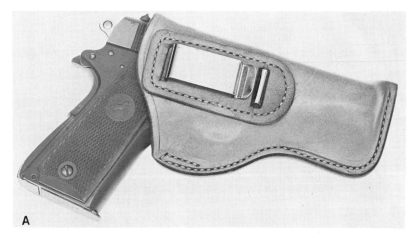

A

Figure 36A. Belly Holster. An in-the-belt holster with a metal clip for holding the gun in position on the belt. This holster can be positioned for a cross draw. Even large guns, such as the Colt Commander, may be carried comfortably and with an excellent concealment factor. Holster is by Bacon Holsters of Rosemead, California.

effective concealment.

CROSS-DRAW HOLSTERS: At one time, these rigs were scorned because an opponent could pin the officer's arm at close range and prevent successful completion of a draw, but they are now gaining popularity because of the many problems with police and automobiles.

Detectives, off-duty officers, and the uniformed officer alone in a one-man radio car have been disarmed by suspects or criminals while sitting in an automobile with weapons holstered on the right side. Other officers, on and off duty, could

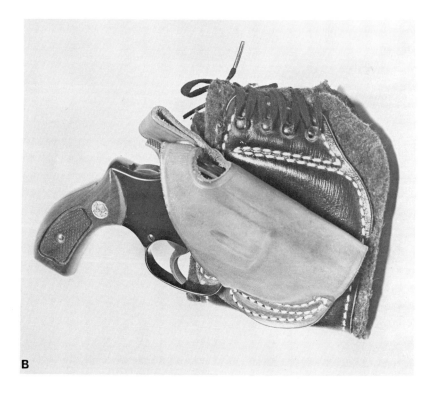

B

Figure 36B. Ankle Holster. The small snub-nosed revolvers, such as the Smith and Wesson Chiefs Special can be concealed effectively in an ankle holster. Leg harness and thumb-break holster shown were made years ago by Gaylord of New York City. They are now available from several manufacturers in the same style. (Gaylord is no longer in the holster business.)

not get their revolvers into action without difficulty because of the cramping of the weapon between the seat of the car and their thigh or leg area.

A cross-draw rig permits an officer to drive a motor vehicle with his body fully between his weapon and any other passenger in the vehicle (let's forget about left-handed cops). If his right arm is pinned down by an assailant (or he is left-handed)

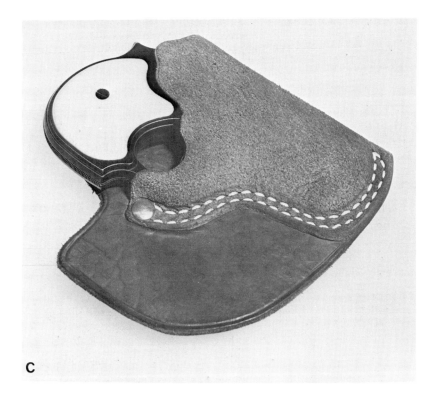

C

Figure 36C. Pocket Hideout Holster. This hideout rig was also made by Gaylord for the ultimate concealment of a small gun with adequate availability when the wearer needed the weapon. The holster back piece is of stiff leather. When fitted into the side trousers pocket, the projection of the back piece (at the butt of gun) catches in the upper lining of the pocket and allows the gun to be slipped out by the wearer's fingers. The gun shown is also the ultimate in concealment: the two-shot derringer in .22 Magnum caliber by High Standard Manufacturing Company, Hamden, Connecticut.

the weapon can be drawn equally well with the left hand from a cross-draw position. If the officer wishes to get into immediate action, he can draw with his right hand and as soon as the muzzle clears the holster (and his left arm), he can fire at opponents outside the driver's window. If the action is to his right front, he can draw with his left hand and fire through the window to his right — keeping his finger oft the trigger (and holding his breath) while the muzzle is crossing his lower pelvic area.

HOLDOUT HOLSTERS: These are designed for maximum concealment and utilize the Smith and Wesson Chiefs Special or the small-butt Colt in a 2-inch barrel length. They are not adapted to concealing larger guns (Fig. 36). These holsters allow an officer to be frisked and not have to give up his or her weapon. However, they also afford some accessibility when the officer draws the gun.

GUNBELTS

While it might never be so recognized, because of the many strange combinations of belts and holsters encountered in any police unit, the gunbelt is an integral part of the gun rig — along with the holster — whenever a belt is used to support a weapon.

A poor fit between a belt and a holster creates two basic faults: (1) the entire rig "gives" as the gun is being drawn until the slack has been taken up, and this is lost time when the gun is not moving out of the holster; and (2) the holster swivels as the gun is being drawn and effectively destroys any directional draw for which the holster might have been designed. When this swiveling forces an officer to draw in a direction away from his normal arc of swinging into a hip shooting position he or she becomes a victim of lost time — moving but not accomplishing much in the way of getting into action. If the swiveling presents the butt of the gun in an unfamiliar position, it may not only slow the draw but might cause the officer to miss the butt entirely — or at least prevent getting a proper grip.

A collateral fault akin to swiveling occurs when the belt is so thin that the holster "walks." This is most common with hip holsters, but it can happen to cross-draw holsters as well. The greatest hazard is that an officer reaches for the gun, but it is not where it's supposed to be, and he has to grope for it. This means lost time, and it could be fatal.

Belts with a thickness adequate to the beltloop of the holster are the best answer.

Modern, thin, dress belts look fine but are not suited to carrying a gun. A belt for small guns, weighing 21 ounces or less, should be at least 3/4 inch in width and preferably 1 inch wide. Guns of heavier weight and with longer barrels require at least a belt measuring 1 1/4 inches in width.

Belts can be stiffened by adding leather to the inside of the belt on the side away from the holster. This slight additional weight seems to make the gun side of the belt slightly lighter and stiffens the entire rig against a difficult-to-reduce "give" on the side of the belt opposite the holster when a gun is drawn quickly.

Conclusion

A holster and gunbelt are vital accessories in combat shooting. The assignment and type of duty to be performed by an officer determines the type of belt and holster to be worn. While the security of the weapon is a factor in considering all holsters, the ease of releasing any safety devices and their simplicity must also be considered. There has to be a rapid-draw potential in all police holsters, and this capability cannot be blocked by elaborate or poorly designed safety devices.

Chapter 12

RELOADING

FACTORY ammunition is expensive, and commercially reloaded ammunition is more costly than reloading. When a reloader can recover bullet metal from a range, it is possible to reload at little out-of-pocket expense.

Police units can buy sufficient amounts of factory ammunition to recover enough empty cases to initiate a program, then purchase bullet metal for their first reloading sessions, and later utilize the bullet metal recovered from the backstop of the pistol range.

Either the police officer or unit can save money by reloading and thus practice much more often on the same budgetary allowance. In combat shooting, practice is a vital element in training.

Cartridges can be reloaded in any of the calibers common to police combat weapons. Revolver cartridges are the most simple reloading operation. In many cases, .38 Special cartridges can be used in place of .357 Magnum cartridges, despite the fact the service weapon of a police agency may be the .357 Magnum. Reloaded ammunition for automatic pistols may present some problems in feeding from the magazine into the chamber.

The start of any reloading program by a police agency or an individual police officer is empty "brass" — fired cartridge cases. Once-fired cases are the best, but most cases can be safely reloaded several times.

Instructions accompanying the various reloading tools detail how these machines take out the fired primers (decapping), insert a new primer (capping), resize the cartridge case, and seat and crimp the bullet into place. Placing the powder in the case may be a separate operation, as is the casting, sizing, and lubricating of bullets.

Reloaded ammunition should be used only on the practice

range. Only factory ammunition should be used in the field.

RELOADING TOOLS

There is a great deal of work to reloading cartridges, but it can be minimized by purchasing reloading tools keyed to the production of reloads in quantity. Low-cost reloading machines are slow, they require handling the cartridge case more than once, and a few require handling at each of the basic operations of decapping, capping, case sizing, "belling" the mouth of the case in preparation for bullet seating, seating the bullet, and crimping the bullet into place. Progressive loading machines are expensive but only require handling the cartridge case once. The progressive reloading tool requires the shooter to insert the case into the machine and keep the machine supplied with primers, powder, and bullets. A progressive reloading tool delivers one completely reloaded cartridge for each movement of the operating level.

Most progressive machines are manually operated, but a few police agencies and most of the commercial reloaders have electrically operated machines.

Reloading requires little more than the reasonable exercise of care. Any work with gunpowder demands care. Accidents can happen while reloading, and they can happen on the practice range because care was not exercised in the reloading room.

With progressive reloading tools, it is difficult but not impossible to put a double — or other excessive — charge of powder in a case. Less sophisticated equipment places the major responsibility on the individual reloading to avoid throwing an excessive amount of powder into a case. The first safeguard is care in using the powder measure, and the second is a visual examination of the filled cases before the bullets are seated in the case.

Double bullets cause a detonation instead of an explosion when a cartridge is fired because they drastically reduce the space in the cartridge case in which pressure can build up. Placing one bullet on top of a completed cartridge and overcoming the crimp of the first bullet as the second one is forced into the case is possible, but it is a highly unusual incident and a happening that must — and can with normal care — be prevented.

CASTING BULLETS

Bullet moulds date from the time people stopped throwing stones. Today's mould is a work of top craftsmanship with multiple cavities. These cavities are reamed out with a tool in the shape of the bullet the mould is to reproduce. The lubricating grooves, the crimping groove, and the face of the bullet are carefully cut into the mould so that the resultant casting is slightly larger than the "as-fired" diameter of the bullet.

A mould is made in two halves with a simple hinge and two long handles. The two blocks that constitute the mould are center pivoted to permit some movement, and a simple pin in each block aligns with a hole in the other half of the mould so that the cavities are perfectly aligned as the mould is closed. The handles are long and end in grips made of wood to reduce the transfer of heat.

A cutoff or sprue plate is hinged to the top of one of the blocks. This plate has a small hole drilled in it for each bullet cavity. These holes are centered over the cavities of the mould when the plate is in the closed position. In gang moulds, these holes are connected by a trough having a narrow elliptical shape, so that the hot lead may be poured directly into this trough, and the metal flows into each of the holes and thus into the cavities of the mould.

At least two gang moulds are desirable for any extensive reloading. The four-cavity mould is ideal for most police officers' muscles. Since most of the work of police is not too muscular, attempts to cast bullets with gang moulds having from six to ten cavities slows down production by tiring out the officers doing the casting. Four-cavity moulds weight little more than a hefty citation book, and officers can work them for hours with little fatigue. Another advantage of the smaller moulds is that standard procedure is to alternate: to pour the hot lead into one mould, then let it cool; knock the bullets out of the other mould, fill it again, place it on the table to cool; and then return and clear the other mould. This permits the lead to cool slowly, and better bullets normally result. In working with a six- or ten-cavity mould, the handloader will find that it cools slowly, at a rate far behind his patience. The result is that the cutoff plate is struck open before the bullets have cooled and lead smears wipe off on the bottom of this plate and on the top of the mould.

The best furnace for heating the bullet metal in preparation for casting bullets is a large-capacity electrically heated furnace.

A small dipper for scooping up the hot lead and pouring it into the trough of the mould is necessary. This dipper should have a long handle ending in a good-sized wood grip.

Many police units have purchased electric furnaces which have a valve and nozzel, and the men working such furnaces do not need a dipper. These valves and nozzles work very well on the larger-capacity furnaces but poorly on the smaller units. The valve may not function due to dirt and other impurities in the molten metal, and the nozzle may clog up with hardened lead due to lack of heat at the nozzle's tip. In either event, time is lost in clearing this malfunction, and sometimes a bad burn may occur. Burns result from attempts to clear the stoppage with a piece of wire from *below* the furnace — when the stoppage clears, the hot lead runs down the wire into the hand of the operator. . .

However, the nozzle and valve feature permits holding a mallet or hammer in one hand continuously and thus speeds up production. The end of the mallet or hammer handle can be used to lift up the handle of the valve to fill the mould with lead and then used in striking open the cutoff plate and clearing the mould.

Bullet metal is an all-encompassing term. The police unit can purchase ingots of bullet metal directly from police equipment and firearm and ammunition supply houses. A desirable alloy for revolver bullets is one part tin to twenty parts lead with some antimony — possibly from one to four parts antimony. In purchasing this material, the officer in charge should purchase a mixture that is not too hard and then on later orders, change over to a harder mixture. The reason for this is that the range lead can be recovered once sufficient firing makes the digging and screening of lead from the backstop worthwhile. This once-fired lead is softened slightly by the heat of firing and the friction of barrel travel, but when mixed with a good hard mixture of bullet metal, it makes fine bullets at low cost.

Hot bullet metal can cause some nasty burns. Therefore, in setting up the furnace for melting the metal, it is highly desirable for the handloader to study out just how fast he can move in the event some of the hot lead lands in his lap — one of the good arguments against casting bullets while sitting down.

The furnace should be so placed that the operator can move away from it without disturbing the stability of the furnace by sudden movements. It should be placed on a solid table or bench which does not tip over at the least pressure. The bench or table should be covered with sheet metal in and around the casting area to protect against fire and to permit easy cleaning of the area when casting is finished for the day.

Water and hot bullet metal do not mix. Keep water away from the furnace, moulds, and dipper. If any water should get into the hot bullet metal, a minor explosion usually results, and a great deal of lead is splashed around. Water is hazardous around a casting operation. It is true that moulds may be cooled in water, but let the experienced handloaders use this technique. It is much safer to use two or three moulds and let them cool by alternating their use.

Moulds can be heated, but never do so by immersing them in hot bullet metal. Again, serious injuries can be sustained. Preheat moulds on or around the furnace, not over direct heat.

Another safety precaution is to have fire-fighting equipment available. You will be working with the makings of a good fire; therefore, be prepared.

Ventilation is very important for the health of officers; the smoke from melting metal can cause any number of minor complaints. Work near an open window at least and, preferably, under a good exhaust-type ventilating fan.

After the elementary safety precautions are completed, the

operator should turn on the furnace and place several ingots of bullet metal in it. At this time, it is a good idea to place the two moulds on the top and sides of the furnace so that they may preheat slightly. The heat of the furnace must be sufficient to melt the bullet metal to a point where it pours like water. Low heat only melts the metal to a fudgelike consistency that does not flow into the cavities of the mould. All the operator gets is a good troughload of metal on the cutoff plate. If the furnace is not equipped with a heat controller, it is possible to test the heat by throwing a half-inch fragment of newspaper on the top of the molten metal. The manner in which the fragment chars or burns tells you whether the metal is ready for casting. Usually, a good dry paper fragment chars and burns rapidly when the metal is hot enough for casting bullets. Using a dipper to scoop up and pour some of the metal also indicates whether the lead is heated sufficiently to have the desirable fluidity.

When the molten metal is ready for casting, a small piece of wax is dropped into the pot, or the surface of the molten metal is touched lightly with a candle. After fluxing with wax, the mixture is then stirred with the dipper. This treatment causes some gases to form, which some operators promptly ignite with a match just above the pot in order to clear the air, but if the ventilation is sufficient, this procedure is not necessary. This fluxing with wax improves the fluidity of the bullet metal and reduces slag. The dross — a dull, sandy substance floating on top of the molten metal, should be cleared from the top of the pot after fluxing with wax.

Gloves are necessary to protect against burns. Lead is heavy even when it is hot, and whenever it lands on a surface, it not only burns, it burns down.

A box should be arranged so that the bullets will be cushioned in their fall from the mould by a small pillow, a slanting piece of board covered with cloth, or some such arrangement. It is important that the bullets land in the box when ejected from the mould in such a way that the impact is lessened; otherwise the bullets will be pushed out of shape. Remember that the bullets are still quite hot and fairly malleable at this stage of the casting process. It is for this reason that handloaders are cautioned to hold the mould as close to the bullet box as possible when ejecting cast bullets. The greatest damage results when the base of the bullet is nicked or dented from impact upon falling into the bullet box or in rolling into another bullet upon landing in the box. Such bullets must be rejected upon inspection.

A small mallet or hammer handle is also necessary to clear the mould. Rawhide mallets work very well but are expensive. Rubber mallets melt when in contact with the mould and stink.

All bullets must be inspected after casting — and after cooling. Any deformation that destroys the distribution of weight within the projectile is reason for rejection and return to the furnace for another try. A "snake" along one side, an incomplete nose, or such deformation means that a bullet will lose its delicate balance in flight and, therefore, cannot be fired with accuracy. Bullets with "fins" along the sides or upon the base should be discarded, as they put a stress upon the die of the sizing tool, and this additional metal is sometimes trapped by the lubricant in one of the grooves, thus imparting an undesirable off-center weight influence to the spinning bullet.

The base and the edges of a bullet are given a close examination. This is a vital area, and any unevenness from holes or depressions in the base to dents or nicks on its edges, call for rejection.

As an operator gains experience, it is possible to inspect bullets as they are cast — as they are flipped from the mould — and thus determine whether the bullet metal and moulds are at the correct temperatures.

Bullets "as-cast" are a few thousandths of an inch larger than the desired diameter, and a sizer and lubricator is necessary to strip off the excess lead and "size" to an exact diameter. Tools of this type most suited to police production of handloaded cartridges are those designed so that the bullets are sized and lubricated with one motion of the machine lever. The bullets are placed into position, the lever actuated once, and the sized and lubricated bullet falls out of the machine.

Once the bullets are sized and lubricated, they should not be "poured" into other containers. Bullets should be lifted individually from the box into which they have fallen from the sizer and lubricator, and the base should be wiped free of lubricant by "stroking" across a piece of cloth stretched across the top of a table or bench. Cardboard separators can be used between layers of bullets so that a cigar box or a metal tray holds several layers of bullets. Trays or boxes should be covered to protect bullets from dust or dirt which might damage the bore of a weapon.

Pouring bullets into containers may nick or dent the base of the bullet — a vital area when accuracy is desired in handloaded ammunition. It may also cause some of the lubricant in the grooves or upon the side of a bullet to be wiped off upon the base of another bullet as they roll together.

Grease on the base of a bullet picks up powder grains from the cartridge when the bullet is seated and the handloading operation is completed. These grains of powder pick up sufficient moisture from contact with the lubricant to ruin their ignition qualities, and this causes varying points of impact due to variations in the powder charge. Therefore, the base of the bullet must be wiped clean upon storage, and a good rule to follow is to once again "stroke" a bullet across a rag to clean its base just as the bullet is being inserted into the top of a cartridge case for the final seating operation.

Bullets can be purchased, but since the entire concept of reloading is based on economy, this expenditure is difficult to justify unless the reloading concerns 9 mm or .45 ACP cartridges and cast bullets cause malfunctions in the automatic pistols on the range.

Chapter 13

PLANNED PRACTICE

P LANNED practice consists of shooting with the empty gun (dry shooting) and firing on a range with live ammunition.* Of course, dry shooting lacks any sustaining interest, and many police officers cannot maintain interest in it. It is a lot more interesting to fire on a range. Dry shooting, however, can help every shooter — both the highly skilled shot and the beginner. It must be intelligent practice with some plan, as mere practice itself only strengthens the muscles.

In planning practice, the police officer should integrate his sessions of dry shooting with range practice. In one, he or she prepares for the other: On the range the officer profits from dry shooting, and during dry practice, faulty habits diagnosed from "reading the target" on the range can be worked out.

Both dry shooting and range firing should be progressive: Each session consists of a certain number of shots and the manner in which they will be fired, and as the sessions progress, they move from the simple to the more difficult techniques of fire — from the fundamentals to advanced principles of shooting.

The plan for each session should be pointed toward correcting some fault or stressing some particular type of fire. If the shooter has scheduled sixty shots for one session, only sixty shots will be fired; the shooter will quit at the end of his scheduled number of shots, even though he may feel like continuing. Too much practice should never be scheduled for any one session: It is a sure way of losing interest.

A beginning shooter finds it difficult to compress the time necessary to learn to shoot. Actually, it is more a case of devel-

---

*About 20 to 30 percent of range firing can be with .22 caliber weapons. This subcaliber practice conserves larger-caliber ammunition and affords excellent practice. However, too much subcaliber practice is not desirable, as policemen must get used to the whip and report of their large-caliber weapons.

oping little-used muscles during the initial stages than it is a question of coordination. As the ability of a shooter to "hold" improves, so does his coordination. For this reason, it is safe to say that a minimum of six weeks elapses before a shooter is usually satisfied with the results of his practice. This is based on three to six dry shooting sessions each week and one to three times on the range. An accelerated course, with at least three times a week on the range and six dry shooting sessions, shows results in two weeks.

BASIC TRAINING COURSE

The basic training is a diversified course, working from slow through timed to rapid fire, and is to be fired at 25 yards on the bull's-eye target, with dry shooting simulating this range practice as much as possible. Students must practice on the range at least once and preferably twice a week, with the two days being well separated, i.e. Tuesday and Friday.

"Calling the shot" is a term used when the shooter attempts to estimate where the bullet hit on the target. The shooter notes just where the front and rear sights (aligned with each other) were at the moment the revolver is fired: high, low, to the left, right, etc., and then checks visually (usually through a telescope or binoculars) where the bullet hit on the target. In coach and pupil shooting, the pupil calls the shot to the coach, who scopes the shot or examines the target. If the bullet hit where it was "called," then trigger jerking or flinching is not one of the shooter's faults, but if it hit in any of the "normal" jerking and flinching areas — and away from your "call," then the trigger was actuated incorrectly. To a lesser degree, the calling of a shot may also indicate incorrect sighting and aiming habits. The pattern of hits on the target, in relation to the calls, is interpreted (Fig. 37).

It should be noted that about 50 percent of the dry firing is on a plain piece of white paper, about letter size. The shooter not only learns to line up his sights properly on this plain target, but also learns to watch them at the instant the hammer falls. It also serves to teach area aiming and prevents the

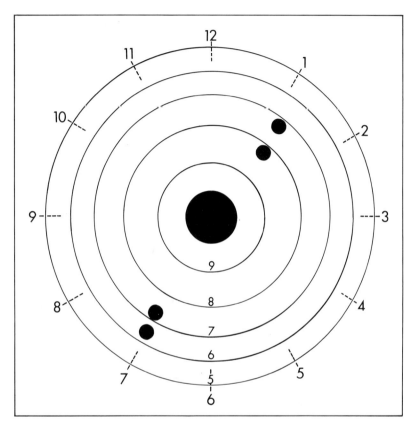

Figure 37. Calling the Shot. Using the standard clock face as a reference, the shooter sounds off as a shot is fired with its expected location on target: "A high eight at one o'clock." "Well out at seven o'clock." When the call and the actual point of impact vary, the coach and pupil discuss possible faults, or reasons for inaccuracy. The two shots shown at one o'clock are in the traditional area of *heeling* (pushing forward with the heel of the hand in anticipation of recoil). The two shots low and left are in the area in which right-handed shooters commonly jerk shots. Failure to watch the sights through the entire trigger motion may land a shot anywhere on target, but always away from where called. This calling of shots may be adapted to the silhouette target, using the same clock method to locate calls.

shooter from becoming "bull's-eye conscious." Such pieces of plain paper can be pasted over the bull's-eye target to blot out the black center at several of the range sessions, if time permits.

It is excellent practice for combat shooting, as the silhouette targets used in combat training also lack any aiming point such as a bull's-eye.

Session	*Dry shooting*	*Range Practice*
First Week	Five ten-shot strings of slow fire, stress being laid on sight alignment and a steadily increasing trigger pressure. Target to be a plain piece of letter-sized paper.	Two ten-shot strings slow fire. Emphasis on safe handling of gun.
Second Week	Same number of shots, same points stressed, but using a bull's-eye target.	Three ten-shot strings slow fire. Practice calling the shot.
Third Week	Twenty shots slow fire, forty shots timed fire. Same points stressed, plain target.	Three ten-shot strings slow fire and one ten-shot string at timed fire (twenty seconds for each string of five rounds).
Fourth Week	Twenty shots slow fire, forty timed fire, and forty rapid fire. Same points stressed, slow and time fire on the bull's-eye target, rapid fire on the plain target.	Two ten-shot strings of slow fire, two ten-shot strings of timed fire, and one five-shot string of rapid fire (ten seconds for five rounds).
Fifth Week	Ten shots slow fire, twenty time fire, and eighty rapid fire, all on bull's-eye target. Stress put on sight alignment, grip pressure, and manipulation of the trigger in both double and single action.	One ten-shot string of slow-fire, three ten-shot strings of timed fire, and one string of rapid fire.
Sixth Week	Ten shots slow fire, twenty time fire, ninety rapid fire. Same points stressed as in fifth week. Bull's-eye target.	One ten-shot string of slow fire, two ten-shot strings of timed fire, and two ten-shot strings of rapid fire.

PRACTICAL PISTOL COURSE

The Practical Pistol Course (PPC) is usually termed the *FBI course,* because it was developed by this fine organization for the training of their own agents. It has proven to be one of the giant forward steps in the history of police marksmanship training. As part of the FBI service program for local police, the personnel of FBI training units instruct local officers in the techniques of combat fire over this reality-tested course of fire.

The PPC teaches a police officer to attain maximum practical effectiveness in minimum time.

Safe handling of the revolver is stressed throughout this course, and every safety precaution must be observed while firing, or range officers direct the officer to cease fire and score his target as "no hits."

The essence of the Practical Pistol Course is the fact that the shooter assumes he is under fire from an armed opponent at all times. He not only must seek to diminish his target area by adopting defensive firing positions but must also race against a time limit. Barricades (any convenient 2 x 4 timber or other support) are utilized at the 25- and 50-yard stages of this course so that the shooter learns to seek protection as he fires and while reloading his gun.

As originally conceived, a shooter "ran" the PPC using divergent and well-separated firing lanes. Practical aspects of range management led to modification of the PPC.

Currently, the PPC is usually divided into elements based upon distances from the target, and appropriate time limits are set for each stage of fire. This makes it possible to move shooters through the course of fire as a group (and with some range discipline), rather than permitting them to run as individuals in the old PPC.

The current course of fire used by police officers competing in combat shooting matches is an excellent modification of the PPC. This course is fired in four stages as follows:

1. 7-yard line; twelve rounds; double action point-shoulder; 25 sec.
2. 25-yard line; eighteen rounds; double action; 90 sec.
   a. Six rounds kneeling
   b. Six rounds left-hand barricade
   c. Six rounds right-hand barricade
3. 50-yard line; twenty-four rounds, double or single action; 2 min., 45 sec.
   a. Six rounds sitting
   b. Six rounds prone
   c. Six rounds left-hand barricade

d. Six rounds right-hand barricade

4. 25-yard line; six rounds; double action off-hand; 12 sec.

All times and commands are given by the rangemaster and include a one-second starting and a one-second ending whistle. There is a thirty-second warning given prior to the termination of time at the 25- and 50-yard line phases.

A total of sixty cartridges (rounds) are fired; targets are combat silhouettes (B-27 or B-27A). *Off-hand* means without support other than the hands of the shooter.

The *California Combat Course* calls for the shooter to fire a total of sixty cartridges (rounds), and to shoot in the barricade position at both 25 and 50 yards with the weak as well as the strong hand.

Too often police officers have excused their lack of ability by explaining that their department did not have a "combat" range. Now, this splendid course of fire makes it possible for many officers to practice combat shooting on a regular pistol range with safety and efficiency.

CUSTOM STOCKS (GRIPS)

Custom stocks or grips, as they are commonly termed, should not be purchased until a shooter has had some experience on the range and has attained a qualifying level of marksmanship. At this stage of a shooter's development, he can evaluate his problems and make a more or less valid decision.

Normally, a factory-issue grip covers the grip of the revolver even with the metal surfaces of the gun's grip. Grips of automatic pistols usually cover a lesser area than the dimensions of the grips of these guns.

Most custom grips are made for revolvers. Particularly with combat automatic pistols, there is not too much that can be done to customize the grip. Figure 38 illustrates the major aspects of custom grips.

In removing factory-issue grips from handguns, do not damage them or the metal surfaces of the gun by attempting to pry them off with a screwdriver or other pointed tool. The proper way to remove grips is to loosen the screw holding them

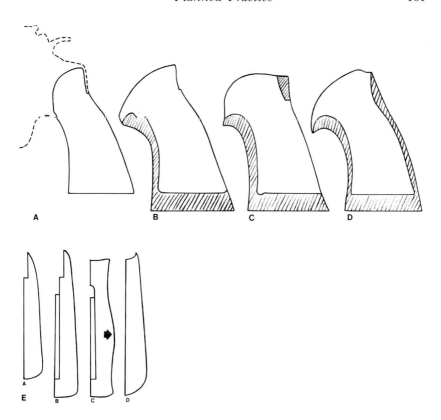

Figure 38. (A) Standard grips by Smith and Wesson (Springfield, Massachusetts) as furnished with their revolvers. Dimensions are the metal outline of the revolver's grip. (B) Smith and Wesson Target® grips have larger dimensions, wood being added where shaded: behind the trigger guard to fill in the gap created by the need for gun designers to plan the standard grip for very large hands and in front of and at the bottom of the grip to offer more hand-contact surface for the shooter. (C) Mustang® custom-designed grips by Mustang Pistol Grips (Temecula, California) have generous proportions, although one size fits most shooters. Wood has been added to fill in the trigger-guard gap, at the top of the grip at the rear and to build a palm swell on the outside of the grip (on the side of the shooter's strong hand: left or right). One helps smother recoil; the other eliminates ride-up upon recoil. (D) Pachmayr (Los Angeles, California) grips completely enclose the revolver's metal-grip frame, adding new dimensions all around. While all the grips described above are checkered walnut, Pachmary grips are checkered "live" rubber. This material offers a no-slip gripping surface and tends to smother recoil of the larger-caliber handguns. (E) Edge views of the above grips show thickness of each grip (A-D). Note palm swell of the Mustang grip (indicated by arrow).

in place about three or four full turns, then to push downward with the tip of the screwdriver on the screw head. This pressure loosens the bottom grip from the gun about 1/8 inch. Continue to loosen the screw until it can be lifted out; slip a thumbnail under the bottom grip and remove it; and then turn the gun over and tap out the other grip with the screwdriver (from the inside; marks are not visible when grips are in place).

COMPETITION AND ACTUAL COMBAT

Try not to shoot alone. Most outdoor ranges are in remote areas, and any accident can be fatal if no one is present to give first aid and seek adequate assistance.

Good safety habits generally eliminate accidents, but where guns and ammunition are mixed, the potential for accidents is always present and should be recognized.

A fellow shooter can serve as coach, and you can help him. This coach-and-pupil method has been utilized by the armed forces to good effect for many years. It is ideal for calling-the-shot practice. In addition, it can be the start of some competition. Whatever fire may be attempted, try to put it on a personal, duel-like basis. If either officer far outshines the other in ability, they should bargain as to a suitable handicap to make the competition more even and stick to that handicap for that day. Fight to beat the other shooter; this is the key to improvement in combat shooting and is also the key to success in later combat situations with criminal opponents.

Later, look around for some other shooter with equal ability and challenge him or her to shoot the course with you. If several officers are shooting together, pick a team and challenge another group of officers in the same department. As improvement is shown with this practice, reach out to nearby departments. What you are striving for is competition, because it tests your ability to shoot under pressure and it needs learning. Competitive shooters term the tendency to shiver and shake and do wrong things under pressure the "big jitters." Hunters term it "buck fever." Conditioning — the experience of doing something over and over again — is the only answer. Look for matches over the PPC course. Each month, more of these combat shoots are being staged by local police. This is the ideal technique of learning how to shoot under pressure in positions which you would also use in combat.

Hope that in your lifetime as a peace officer you never have to defend yourself or any one in your company from the fire of a criminal opponent. Also, be certain you can shoot fast and accurately under the pressure of hot lead and discharge your obligations to your community, your family, and yourself.

APPENDICES

NOMENCLATURE — REVOLVER

The names of the various major parts of a revolver and their location are indicated in the following list and the diagram in Figure 39:

1. Front sight
2. Barrel
3. Ejector
4. Cylinder
5. Frame
6. Trigger guard
7. Trigger
8. Rear sight
9. Hammer
10. Hammer spur
11. Cylinder latch
12. Grip
13. Backstrap
14. Butt

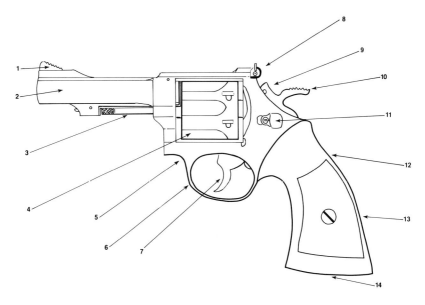

Figure 39.

Appendix B

NOMENCLATURE — AUTOMATIC PISTOL

The names of the various major parts of an automatic pistol and their location are indicated in the following list and the diagram in Figure 40:

1. Front sight
2. Barrel
3. Barrel bushing
4. Slide
5. Receiver
6. Slide stop
7. Trigger guard
8. Trigger
9. Magazine release
10. Ejection port
11. Rear sight
12. Hammer
13. Safety (thumb)
14. Safety (grip)
15. Main spring housing
16. Grip

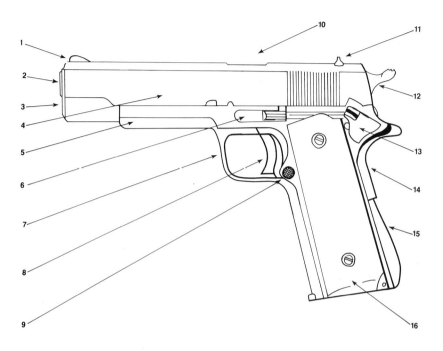

Figure 40.

INDEX